# Praise for the Dating Goddess

The Adventures in Delicious Dating After 40 series of books is based on the blog Adventures in Delicious Dating After 40 at www.DatingGoddess.com. Here are comments from readers.

♥ "Adventures in Delicious Dating After 40 is a wonderful composite of both the mechanics of post-40 online dating and what the practice of honoring one's self actually looks like. How marvelous your writing is to read. I spent about 2 hours reading and was riveted the whole time." —Maggie Hanna

♥ "At last, a dating writer who addresses requirements. You are SO right on! I'm thrilled to have found you!" —Rachel Sarah, author, *Single Mom Seeking*

♥ "Powerfully heartfelt and honest writing. You are inspiring." —Kare Anderson, Emmy Award winning writer

"I just love your writing. It is very fresh and gives the reader something to think about." —Kelly Lantz, President & Manager, 55-Alive.com

"Dating Goddess, you are like a, a, a, well, a goddess to me. You've helped guide me successfully through my re-entry into the dating world after 14 years. I'm an eager student and fast study, and do get myself into situations that others don't know how to deal with — such as 3 dates in one day -— so thankfully you are there! You're the greatest, thanks for all you do for us!" —Jae G.

"I find your point of view much more interesting than other dating writers. Thanks for always reminding me to enjoy dating life no matter what it throws at you." —Sandy

"I love Adventures in Delicious Dating After 40. I really do like your honest and authentic voice — it's refreshing." —Wendy S.

"Adventures in Delicious Dating After 40 is really fun to read. Thanks for sharing your thoughts and letting us divorced single women know that we are not alone. There's a lot here that I identify with, although I'm not as brave as you are about dating lots of guys. So far. Love your blog — the first blog I've ever read consistently." —Elizabeth

"Thanks for a wonderful blog. You're doing a great job of saying what's in my mind. There's rarely a day I miss when it comes to checking in on your wisdom." —Paulette Ensign

# First-Rate First Dates

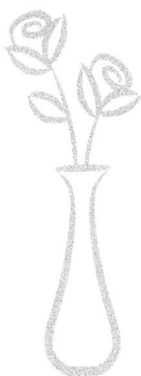

*Increasing the Chances*
*of a Second Date*

by **Dating Goddess**

*First-Rate First Dates: Increasing the Chances of a Second Date*

Second Edition

Cover design by Dave Innis, www.innisanimation.com

Book design by JustYourType.biz

Printed in the United States of America.

ISBN    Print:    978-1-930039-39-1

         eBook:  978-1-930039-18-6

How to order:

The *Adventures in Delicious Daing After 40* books may be ordered directly from www.DatingGoddess.com.

Quantity discounts are also available. Visit us online for updates and additional articles.

*The Adventures in Delicious Dating After 40 books are dedicated to my ex-husband since he unexpectedly released me to explore the untethered life of a single woman. I then had the freedom for the experiences, lessons and insights shared in these pages.*

# Books by Dating Goddess

♥ *Date or Wait: Are You Ready for Mr. Great?*

♥ *Assessing Your Assets: Why You're A Great Catch*

♥ *In Search of King Charming: Who Do I Want to Share My Throne?*

♥ *Embracing Midlife Men: Insights Into Curious Behaviors*

♥ *Dipping Your Toe in the Dating Pool: Dive In Without Belly Flopping*

♥ *Winning at the Online Dating Game: Stack the Deck in Your Favor*

♥ *Check Him Out Before Going Out: Avoiding Dud Dates*

♥ *First-Rate First Dates: Increasing the Chances of a Second Date*

♥ *Real Deal or Faux Beau: Should You Keep Seeing Him?*

♥ *Multidating Responsibly: Play the Field Without Being A Player*

♥ *Moving On Gracefully: Break Up Without Heartache*

♥ *From Fear to Frolic: Get Naked Without Getting Embarrassed*

♥ *Ironing Out Dating Wrinkles: Work Through Challenges Without Getting Steamed*

# Contents

# *Introduction*

This book is designed for anyone who is interested in stories, advice, and lessons from the midlife dating front. If you are over 40 and haven't dated in a while — or even if you have — you'll learn ways to approach dating with zeal, optimism, and hope. Even if you've had more than your share of negative experiences, I'll share how to glean lessons from those adventures, rather than just declaring that "all men are jerks" or "men are just looking for sex."

While most of the perspective is from a woman to women, men's comments, experiences, and lessons have been integrated as appropriate.

This book began as daily entries into my blog, Adventures in Delicious Dating After 40, which has been featured in the *Wall Street Journal* as well as on radio and TV. I wrote about my epiphanies from my and my friends' dating life. The best postings were culled to make this and subsequent books.

This book focuses on what goes on during the first date. We'll explore how to determine if you want a second date as well as what you can do to increase the likelihood your date will ask you for a second — if you want a repeat!

xi

This book consists of three types of perspectives:

*Lessons:* These are specific experiences I thought would be useful to you. A few lines from my experience illustrate the points.

*Insights:* These usually start with an experience I've encountered, then the insights that experience spawned. It is usually comprised of around half story and half insight.

*Stories:* These are examples of situations I've experienced — or was currently experiencing when I wrote that piece — that I thought would be entertaining. Or I thought the story would help you see what kind of things happen in the midlife dating world so you'd know what has happened to others.

Because these writings were real time, as they occured, they are often set in the present tense. But they are not chronological. So a reference to "my current beau" may now be many sweethearts ago. I hope this isn't confusing.

I'd love ot hear your stories and questions. Please email them to me at Goddess@DatingGoddess.com. They may make it into the blog or my next book!

# Who is the Dating Goddess?

I am a middle-aged, white, professional woman. My husband of nearly 20 years left me in April 2003 when I was 47, 11 days shy of 48. After giving my heart time to heal from the surprise divorce sprung by the man I thought was my soulmate, I started dating 18 months later. Generally, I have had a great time meeting interesting men, some of whom became romantic beaus, some became treasured friends, and some I never heard from again.

> *I am not a well-preserved, gorgeous, marathon-running middle-aged women*

In the beginning, I had dates with single male colleagues, but I quickly found Internet dating was the way to explore the most "inventory" and qualify men who I thought might be a good match.

I am not one of those well-preserved, gorgeous,

marathon-running middle-aged women. I have been told I am attractive, but I am overweight and not a gym rat. So while I am active, I do not match the description 90% of men's profiles say they want: slender, athletic, toned, fit. I have some wrinkles — what one sweet suitor mistakenly called dimples. I have what Bridget Jones called "wobbly bits," as most non-surgically enhanced middle-aged women do. My genes — and a lifetime addiction to chocolate — have made their mark. Yet I've met and dated some wonderful men, so even if you're not a lingerie model, you can find guys who will think you're attractive, perhaps even hot!

In my professional life, I am a bestselling author of workplace effectiveness books, professional speaker and management consultant. I've appeared on Oprah, 60 Minutes, and National Public Radio and in the *Wall Street Journal* and *USA Today*.

This book is intended to not only be useful to others and cathartic for me, but is also the genesis of a new topic for fun, thought-provoking speeches. I'm calling myself a dating philosopher and giving date-a-vational speeches! Let me know if you know a group who would like an entertaining after-lunch speech on how lessons learned from dating have implications in business and personal relationships and well as life philosophies.

How did I come by the Dating Goddess moniker? After a few months of dating dozens of men — one week yielded 7 dates with 6 guys in 5 days — my friends dubbed me this name. I liked it, so it stuck.

I'm purposefully not sharing my picture as I don't want you to think either, "How did she get any dates at all?" or the opposite, "Of course she found it easy to get 112 men to ask her out." I am not hideous (usually) nor am I stunning (without professional hair, makeup and Photoshop!). Some men find me attractive, some don't.

I continue to search for my "one," but I have learned a lot along the way, and my single and not-single friends have loudly encouraged me to share my experiences and lessons in the hopes of helping others navigate the adventure of dating with more success. And to have a delicious time doing it!

# *Start with coffee*

New online daters have shared that they are concerned about accepting a date with someone and as soon as they meet him, they know he is not a match. If the plan is for dinner, dancing, lunch or hiking, they know they are in for hours of making polite conversation with someone they know is not their type.

The solution: Start with coffee.

If you have not met this man, no matter how charming and fun he sounds on the phone or in emails, start with coffee. If you meet and hit it off, coffee can easily extend to lunch or dinner. I've had 5-hour dates that started with coffee and went into a meal.

Coffee is a minimal time investment: 30 minutes to an hour. You can be polite to nearly anyone for 30 minutes, can't you? Even if you meet and know there is no attraction, fight the urge to exit after 5 or 10 minutes. Unless he is totally offensive, stick it out for 30 minutes. You may make a new pal, or have a gal pal with whom he might be a good match.

I've dissuaded guys who wanted to start with dinner and dancing. I've learned from experience. I now say

"Let's start with coffee and see if we hit if off and want to spend more time together. Then our second date can be that nice dinner you're suggesting." They understand and agree.

If you want to meet after work, a drink would seem logical. However, it is a tad awkward as it gets toward dinner time to decline an offer of dinner if he thinks it is going well. But if you want to bail, don't do dinner. Extricate yourself as gracefully as possible: "I'm sorry, I must be going." "I have a big day tomorrow, so want to get ready for it tonight."

This is why coffee is the perfect solution. For some reason it is less of a problem to leave when your coffee cup is drained. So don't set up yourself to suffer — agree to start with coffee.

# *How do you greet him?*

When I first started dating, I asked my dating friends, "How do you greet someone upon first meeting?" Shaking hands seems too businesslike. Doing nothing seems cold and aloof.

I've settled on a quick hug. Since I've often been flirting with potential suitors by phone and email for at least a few days if not a week or more, I feel they aren't strangers. Heck, if I'm at a church service, I hug people with whom I've had much less contact!

Hugging also shows you're affectionate and not afraid of contact. Just don't linger too long, or it might send a message you don't want to send!

If I feel particularly fond of the person from our emails and calls, I'll kiss him on the check. I've not had anyone seem offended by this greeting.

And at the end of the encounter, unless it was unpleasant, I always give him a quick hug too. Longer if we really hit it off, and often a kiss on the cheek. But don't be too affectionate if you don't want to see him again. I've found even a hug for a pleasant encounter can cause the guy to think you're more interested than you are.

# Guys make a great first impression with a small gift

A guy's first-date present was a recent bestselling book he thought I'd like. It was a great gift, as it is in the genre I read and hadn't bought yet. Thumbs up!

One guy's first-date gift was a CD of romantic songs to play while cooking together. He said we could play it when we prepare a meal together. Good move — it was thoughtful and suggested a second encounter.

> *It was thoughtful and suggested a second encounter*

The stuffed bear with a red heart was brought to me on Feb. 16. I knew my date bought it half price, but that didn't diminish its effect on me. It was very sweet. The guy who brought it and I are now dear friends, so the bear sits in a special place in my bedroom and I think of him and that first date every time I see it.

One man brought a bouquet of flowers. Another brough one red rose which made him stand out. And another brought flowers, a stuffed bear and a "thinking of you" greeting card!

It's not the gift itself, although if it is a great gift, it's even better. More it shows thoughtfulness, care and that the guy went out of his way to make the first date memorable. So even if there were other parts of the date that were so-so, a small gift will often tip the scale to ensure a second date.

# Good conversation is the foundation of great dating

One of the things that has stood out for me in dating interactions is that many guys don't know how to make conversation. I'm not just talking chit chat, but any kind of give and take.

And that is precisely what is missing — give and take. The men I've talked to recently seem to be missing the how-to-ask-questions gene. While I admit that since I am curious about a lot of things, questions come more easily to me than for some. I've learned to interject comments, stories and tidbits into the conversation lest my potential suitor think he's being interrogated. But most of them don't know how to piggy back on my comments to draw me out or to continue the discussion. They merely turn it back on themselves or talk about what interests them.

I had a dinner date with a man who did a good

job of sharing the initial phone conversation. However, at dinner he did 85% of the talking. When I would interject, my comments just sat there — he didn't ask me anything further. Perhaps my perspective and life weren't interesting to him. That's certainly a possibility. However, many strangers on planes seem more interested in my life than some of the potential dates I've spoken to!

Are they shy? Nervous? Wanting to tell me everything possible in the first interaction? It would be more engaging if they worked to share the air time. They'd have more luck getting second dates — or even first ones — if they were more conscientious about how they converse in the first conversation.

# He had me from "You're gorgeous!"

In "Jerry McGuire," Renee Zellweger's character tells Jerry, "You had me from 'hello.'" Mine was a little different.

We'd talked a few times on the phone and had nice, but brief, conversations. Although we'd exchanged pictures, I had no idea if I'd be attracted to him or him to me. We agreed to meet at a coffee shop after work.

He called from a block away, telling me he'd be there in a minute. When he walked in the door, I waived. A giant grin filled his face. He walked toward me, his arms extended for a hug. I embraced the invitation! His first words: "You're gorgeous!" What a great start!

He was tall, well dressed, nice looking, and bald. Bald is sexy on some men — and it certainly was on him. As the evening progressed, I learned he was funny, intelligent, thoughtful, attentive, chivalrous, insightful, accomplished, humble and well educated.

We laughed, smiled and shared. We got so engrossed in each other we forgot to order coffee. He asked good, interesting questions and listened intently. After asking "Do you like to be touched?" and I responded "Absolutely!" he reached over and took my hand.

After 90 minutes, we walked hand-in-hand down the street and listened to the band playing outside. As we swayed to the music he slipped his arm around my waist. He moved it to the back of my neck, which he tenderly stroked.

He asked if I wanted to have dinner. Yes, I did. While we stood in a corner waiting for the outside table to be cleared, he gently kissed me. Nothing hot and heavy, just a sweet kiss. At the table, he sat in the chair next to me. We held hands throughout dinner.

*I don't have dimples — those are wrinkles*

He told me he liked my dimples. I thanked him. I didn't tell him that I don't have dimples — those are laugh lines, AKA wrinkles! He also said, based on some of my comments, it seemed I wasn't completely happy with the shape of my body. I said yes, that was true, I'd like to lose more weight. He said "I love your body. If you're concerned about any bumps or jiggles, that is what bodies our age are supposed to do." I wanted to run away with him right then.

We were the last couple in the restaurant. As we left, we passed a club with dance music spilling out. He said "Let's check this out," and escorted me inside to the dance floor. Heaven! We had one dance before the band took a break.

He walked me to my car, opening my door, then we lingered in a sweet kiss. He was a gentleman and didn't try to take liberties beyond a kiss. And a great kisser he was! We parted with a promise he'd call the next day. Which he did.

This was one of the very best first dates I've had in a long, long time. And it all started with "You're gorgeous!" Note to self: the first response can set the tone for the whole evening — and beyond. So make sure you respond positively if you have a good initial reaction.

(I also wrote about him in "Falling in lust" in the *Ironing Out Dating Wrinkles: Work Through Challenges Without Getting Steamed* book and "Be creative to get his attention!" in the *Winning at the Online Dating Game: Stack the Deck in Your Favor* book.)

# When it clicks, throw out some of your criteria

I met a wonderful man online 10 days ago. He is successful, intelligent, funny, gentlemanly, worldly, interesting, communicative, educated, considerate, articulate, complimentary, shares his feelings, and is a great conversationalist. So far, we share the values we've discussed. We have similar political views and philosophies about life. We are both small business owners. We talk every day for an hour. But we haven't met. Why?

*He lives 2000 miles away*

Because he lives 2000 miles away.

I nearly never communicate with a man outside a 1-hour drive from my home. Why? Because I've found

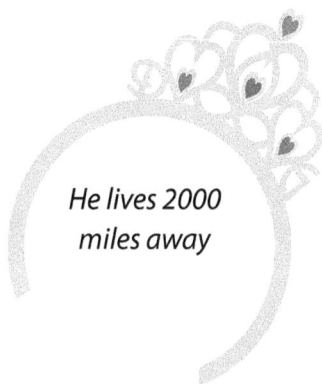

it takes being with a man to really see how I feel around him. How does he treat me when we're together? It's easy to be charming and chivalrous on the phone. It's another thing when he walks five steps ahead or doesn't look me in the eye when he talks.

So far, I really like what I've gotten to know, more so than any other man I've encountered in this dating adventure. We are arranging a time to meet, but we both have extended travel coming up soon. We are looking at connecting in person when we both return.

I'll see if I reassess my no-long-distance-relationship rule. I think this one may be worth ditching the rule for.

(See "Anticipating a big date is like awaiting Santa" in the *Check Him Out Before Going Out: Avoiding Dud Dates* book for the next installment of this story. And "Gentleman morphs into masher" on page 19, for the end.)

# *Tracking your date's score*

A guy begins with 100 units. He can add to these units by doing good things (e.g., calling when he says he will, being chivalrous, suggesting activities he thinks I'd like, bringing small gifts, remembering info from previous conversations), smiling, making me laugh, having a good vocabulary, using proper grammar, dressing in clean, appropriate clothes, having good manners, generally being fun, interested, present and thoughtful.

And yes, looks do count — if he's yummy he gets more points than if he is average. Average-looking guys can come out ahead of a yummy guy by earning points in other areas. And if you find him sexy, then jackpot!

Units are deducted for being late without calling, hogging the conversation, focusing the conversation only on himself, his kids, interests and work, interrupting, not making eye contact, or answering his cell phone without first informing me he's expecting an urgent call. Other demerits are taken for being unkempt (dirty clothes, unshined shoes, wrinkled shirt), being unchivalrous (walking first into/out of a building, not holding the door, walking on the inside of the sidewalk), having poor table manners, mispronouncing too many words, or being unkind to anyone. Moving too fast (hand on my thigh within minutes of meeting me, trying to French kiss too soon, and trying to sleep with me on the first date) is also a big demerit earner.

I don't actually keep score — although I often think I should. I would have to assign values to the various behaviors. For example, being unkind would earn a lot more demerits than unshined shoes. And being kind and thoughtful are awarded a lot more points than walking on the outside of the sidewalk.

But I do notice all of the above and make a mental note. Here's an example from a recent first date.

Good: Often emails fun notes, brought small gift, pleasant to waiter, seemed to pay attention when I talked, had good eye contact, smiled, shared air time, treated for lunch, asked to see me again.

Bad: Walked into restaurant first, didn't hold door for me, took cell phone call during lunch, interrupted a lot.

So what's the net score for this guy? Around 105. His pluses earned him back points he lost. So I'll see him once more, then decide if I want to see him again.

(See "Deciding to see him again or not" in the *Real Deal or Faux Beau: Should You Keep Seeing Him?* book for what happened with this one.)

# Long-distance suitor and the first date

*"Absence makes the heart grow fonder— of somebody else." —Anonymous*

A man who lives 400 miles away has been flirting with me for months and calls every day. He decided he would fly to my city to meet me. He'd get a car and a hotel room, so there would be no discomfort with him wanting to stay with me.

Today he called and said "I have an idea. Why don't you come here? Some weeks ago I'd made plans with the guys to golf at a resort a few hours away and I still have the reservations even though the outing is off. And it would be easier, as I wouldn't have to schlep my golf clubs on the plane to your place."

*Easier on whom?*

A few things immediately crossed my mind. First, easier on whom? Certainly not me, as I'd have to schlep myself (sans clubs) to his place, then be at his mercy unless I rented a car.

Also, this was the first mention of golf. Isn't the whole point of getting together to spend some quality time and see how we like each other? When he's spending one day on the golf course of the two we are together, that limits our getting-to-know-you time.

Then there's staying at the resort. This is our first time meeting. Would he expect to sleep with me? Or do I rent another room? This first encounter was now starting to cost me a pretty penny for a guy who was willing and interested enough in me to come to my city.

I stammered that I would think about it and we could talk about it later today. I will bring up my concerns, especially about sleeping arrangements.

First dates can be hard enough without adding the complications of feeling put out by the arrangements. If I were advising someone else, I'd say save the resort time for later in the relationship when you know you click. I think I'll take my own advice!

# *Gentleman morphs into masher*

I recognized him at the airport coming past Security. He was taller than he seemed in his pics, better looking and better built. He'd flown 13 hours, yet he'd donned a suit and tie because he knew I find men in well-fitting suits sexy!

He recognized me — I was wearing a tiara, of course. He said he'd have recognized me without it. He kissed me on both cheeks — how European! — and gave me a quick hug.

We dropped his suitcases at his hotel and I waited while he changed. His body clock said 5 a.m. so he was tired and hungry. During an enjoyable dinner with good conversation, we periodically touched and held hands, as we had walking to the restaurant. After dinner, he announced he was tired, so we walked back to his hotel.

As we hugged goodbye, he suddenly got a burst of energy. He started kissing and caressing me like a starving man at an all-you-can-eat buffet who voraciously fills his plate to overflowing believing he'll never eat again. It was as if someone had announced "Let the grope-fest begin!" I quickly extricated myself, as I knew where this one-way grab train was heading and I wanted off at the next station.

What happened? How did he go from gentleman to masher in a few minutes? Did I give off unintended signals that I was easy? What happened to decorum on the first date? What happened to respect? Did he think that his airfare and hotel costs entitled him to sex? Did he really expect that I would sleep with him within hours of meeting him? Was he used to that from other women, or was I just so luscious he couldn't control himself? I doubt either was the case.

I was disappointed that I had to fight him off. I didn't see it coming.

We saw each other for a few hours the next day before his flight home. He was back to being a gentleman, albeit an affectionate one. He says he'll return in a month for a longer visit, staying in the same hotel. So at least he doesn't assume he'll stay with me. Before he buys his ticket, we will discuss expectations. If he expects to fly 2000 miles for sex, he shouldn't bother. For the same price he could get a high-priced call girl.

*"Give a man a free hand and he'll run it all over you."* —Mae West

(The rest of the story: I never heard from him again. Not a peep. No emails nor calls. I guess he was put out that I didn't put out.)

# Clues a guy is just looking for a booty call

I asked my friend, the writer of "Male Call," a syndicated newspaper columnist on "Advice From a Guy," a question I thought might interest you. We had this exchange:

**DG:** What are signs a guy is just looking for a booty call on the first date?

**MC:** Wait a sec — who says guys are angling for anything more than a soul-stirring, earnest conversation about their feelings on the very first date?

Just kidding. We want to talk about your feelings, too.

No, but seriously. There are indeed a few things to watch for. One is excessive touching. Remember, it's the first date — shoulder rubs and thigh squeezes are for later in the process — maybe the second date. An offhand, seemingly absentminded brush of her forearm as you're making a point about thermonuclear dynamics is fine. We encourage it, even; it's a subtle sign that you're interested. (But on second thought, leave out the thermonuclear part.)

**DG:** This is good. I've had that thigh squeezing you reference. Also, French kissing within minutes of meeting me, and "accidental" brushes of my breast. I've been tempted to ask "Do I have SLUT tattooed on my forehead?" I've even had guys tell me what positions they envision us in before the night ends. Yuck!

Any other clues, oh wise MC?

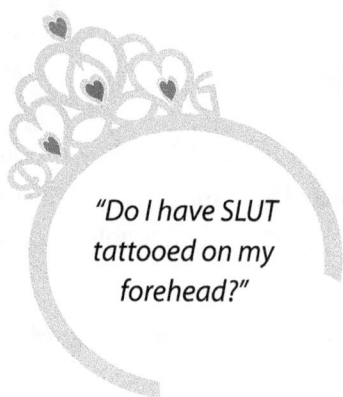

*"Do I have SLUT tattooed on my forehead?"*

**MC:** You've touched on another one: he continually steers the conversation toward something sexual, or at least suggestive. You: "So, have you seen any good movies lately? I loved 'Little Miss Sunshine.'" Him: "Yes, I have! It reminded me of one of my favorite movies, 'Thong Party III.' You know, I happen to have a copy at home. I live just around the corner." Bonus warning tip: He picks a place to meet that happens to be very near his bachelor pad.

**DG:** You are so right, again! I had a guy suggest we go back to his place within minutes of meeting me. And I'm not showing up in cleavage-revealing, tight, short slutware or being provocative. I'd like to think I just have this mojo thing going, but I know it's really more about his having a horny thing going.

Thanks, MC. I guess I know more about this than I thought! But it's always good to hear it directly from a guy.

# 12 signs he won't be asking for a second date

He's pleasant and cordial, not a jerk. But he's showing indications that you won't be dating a second time. Recognize any of these signs?

- You'd agreed to meet for a drink. The waiter brings your drinks, but when he asks if you are ready to order, your date immediately says, "We're just having drinks." If he were interested in spending more time with you, he'd say, "Check back in a little while" or at least offer to order appetizers.

- He doesn't make much eye contact. That means he doesn't like looking at you. Even if he is shy, if a man thinks you're attractive, he won't be able to keep his eyes off you. (Yes, some men don't make eye contact if they think you are stunning. But most will want to ogle.)

- He doesn't comment on your attractiveness. An interested guy says, "You're much prettier than your pictures," or even "Wow! You're beautiful," or "You have such pretty eyes." He'll find something to compliment you on.

💜 No casual touching. If a guy is attracted to you, he'll usually touch your arm or hand, or the small of your back as you walk to the table.

💜 He doesn't smile much. Even if he is shy, a man who wants to make a good impression smiles at what you say and laughs when you attempt something funny.

💜 If the waiter asks if you want another drink, your date doesn't ask you, he just says, "We're fine." Do not, under any circumstances, order another drink unless your date asks you. He wants to be polite, but he can get surly if you make him wait while you down another.

*Do not, under any circumstances, order another drink*

💜 He doesn't seem interested in you. He doesn't ask you questions about your interests or life.

💜 No mention of a second date. An attracted man will try to set up the second date during the first, or at least mention it as a possibility. For example, if you mention something you like (e.g., type of movies, food, music or activity) he'll say, "Next time we will go there/try that."

- He can't wait to get the check. He may chase down the waiter if it isn't coming fast enough.

- He accepts your offer to split the check. Bad sign. This shows he has no interest in you romantically.

- He doesn't walk you to your car.

- He shakes your hand as you part and mumbles something like, "It was nice to meet you." Or as you both walk to the parking lot, he peels off toward his car calling "Take care" with a wave.

Any of these alone doesn't signify no second date. However, if you see several of these signs — or heaven forbid, all of them — just get out of there as quickly and pleasantly as possible.

Don't take it personally. Just know it isn't a match and move on. Next!

# First-date red flags that this guy isn't for you

He's pleasant and cordial. However, there are red flags that make you cautious. Some by themselves are deal breakers (he drinks too much), while others have the cumulative effect of "I'm going to pass on this guy." For each woman the red flags she notices will be different. Here are some of mine:

- **He talks too much.** He doesn't ask you a question, except perhaps a trite one like, "Tell me about yourself." Or, as a recent date kept asking, "So, how are you?" The same as I was 5 minutes ago, but getting more turned off each time you ask!

- **He has poor manners.** He interrupts frequently, orders first, eats non-finger-food (salad, pork chops) with his hands in a nice restaurant, *walks ahead of you, doesn't open doors.*

- **He's poorly dressed for the activity.** He shows up in badly wrinkled shirts or slacks, ripped clothing, poorly kept, unpolished, or filthy shoes, ill-fitting clothes (too big, too small), hair disheveled or dirty, or shorts for a white-tablecloth dinner. While most guys are not clothes horses, they should at least be clean and neat.

*He has trouble keeping eye contact*, seems distracted by nearly everything around him. If he's having this much trouble staying focused, guess what? He'll have trouble staying focused on you in the relationship. Inattention plays out in other ways in a relationship, but I've seen the signs from the beginning with inability to stay focused in the conversation.

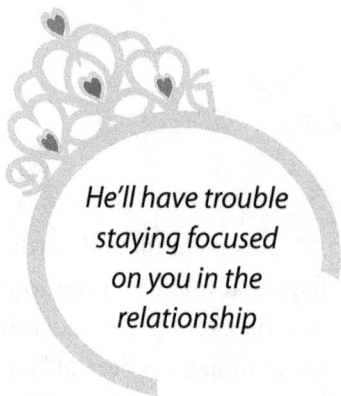

> *He'll have trouble staying focused on you in the relationship*

*He's condescending to service staff.* He is snotty to the waiter, snaps at the clerk, is arrogant with the ticket taker or valet. He doesn't have to act like they are his best friends, but he needs to be pleasant and cordial to everyone with whom he interacts.

*He seems paranoid and negative.* He goes off on how all corporations are colluding to screw consumers, the government reads everyone's email and listens to every phone call, etc. He makes broad negative generalizations about people, women, government, etc. He gets irritated at life's common mishaps of traffic, lines, rude behavior, high prices. Life is too short to be listening to someone's frequent rants.

♥ *He gets sexual way too early.* He tries to French kiss within minutes of meeting you, has his hand on your thigh, talks about how he wants to make love to you in various locations/positions, rubs his body inappropriately on yours, gropes you, at the end of the date he suggests he come home with you or you with him.

♥ *He complains about the women from past relationships.* Or focuses on bad date stories. He's got an ax to grind and issues with women. You don't want to be the one to try to get him to see there are lots of good women out there.

The bottom line is to be aware of the times you feel disappointed with his self-focus, inattention to you, disrespect, or boorish behavior. You can't build a relationship on a foundation of disappointment. You may think other attributes will make up for these disappointments, but while many of them are changeable, do you really want a fix-up-project man?

# Ambivalence

Ambivalence is the bane of the dating world. I've had plenty of unremarkable dates with guys who were smart, educated, successful, and attractive, yet I felt if I saw him again, fine; if not, fine. I debated with myself whether I'd accept a second date or not.

*Why not take the risk of investing a little more time?*

On the one hand, there was nothing odious or off-putting, so why not spend a little more time together and see if a spark gets lit? We can all have off days, so why not take the risk of investing a little more time? If nothing develops after the second date, it's time to cut each other loose and move on.

On the other hand, if I didn't find him scintillating in our first encounter, why waste both our time? You have plenty of other things on your calendar, so investing a little more time means you'd have to give up something else.

What to do?

Two options come to mind.

1.  You can invest a little more time on the phone and see if you're drawn to get together.

2.  You could get together for coffee or something with a short time investment. If no spark, then move on. But maybe by giving him a second chance, the spark will be fanned.

# *Date turned out to be losing bet*

While most daters can regale you with stories of dates gone bad, only about 10% of my dates fall in this category. And even bad dates have had some learning for me. This one helped me create the "only coffee first date" rule (see page 1).

After seeing the movie "Dreamer: Inspired by a True Story," I decided I wanted to see a horse race. Never having been to one, I wanted to go with someone experienced, who could show me the reins — I mean ropes.

A few weeks later I received an email and subsequent phone call from a 41-year-old guy whose profile said he was a "race horse owner." An extremely enthusiastic man, he had more pictures of his horse than of himself in his profile. His enthusiasm wasn't limited to his motivational-speaker style voice tone; nearly every word in his emails started with a capital letter.

He wanted to meet me, so when he mentioned he

was going to the local race track to check out the newest horse phenom, I asked if I could tag along. Normally, I wouldn't have sought a date with a man who didn't meet my age, economic, or articulation criteria, but I wanted a tutor for the races. Sometimes tutoring costs more than you think!

When I was ten minutes away from the track, he called to say he'd be 40 minutes late. He hadn't carefully checked the bus and train schedule and had missed his connection. I had considered taking the train myself, as there is a station on the track grounds, so I didn't think this too odd, although I was mildly miffed he hadn't looked into this beforehand.

He said he was wearing a black cowboy hat and tweed coat. As I sat outside the entrance watching arriving train passengers enter, a tall man with that attire entered. But he looked less attractive than Mr. Race-HorseOwner's picture, so I let him pass. A few minutes later he called. Yep, that was him. Sigh. I went inside to meet him.

We set about getting a lay of the land. It seems he'd only been to the races once before, so really didn't know much more than me. So much for my race mentor!

We began with lunch. He stabbed his whole meat loaf slab with his fork and raised it to his mouth — without cutting it beforehand! It landed on the shelf his protruding belly made under his white shirt. Ugh! I was reminded of his lack of table manners every time I looked at him the rest of the afternoon — a brown meat loaf stain staring out at me from his midriff paunch.

During lunch he shared that his transportation is "BMW" — which he explained is "bus, Muni and walking." No car. He also disclosed he still lived at home. How can a 41-year-old man living with his mother and with a full-time job not have a car in our area where a car is nearly a requirement?

When I asked about his race horse, he explained that he owns 1/100th a share. Yes, that is right — there are 99 other owners! So while "race horse owner" sounds successful and enticing in his profile, the truth is different.

I endured an afternoon of bad grammar, wrong word usage, incorrect pronunciation, and repeating himself. He is a college grad, but he would be a poor advertisement for his alma mater!

There were a number of times I felt like leaving, but the star horse had yet to run. While it was good to see a race with a soon-to-be-famous horse in it, it was not worth six hours of my life. And to make matters worse, since we were both novices at betting, we bet wrong and didn't even make money on the horses we thought we had bet on!

My lesson: before agreeing to spend the afternoon with someone, make sure it's someone with whom I want to spend time. And yes, it was my own fault for trying to turn a date into a tutoring session, even though he was a willing teacher. Little did I know he didn't know enough to be an informed instructor.

Make sure to download your free
eBook Attract Your Next Great Mate:
Dating Advice From Top Relationship Experts at www.DatingGod-
dess.com/freebie

# Dr. Jekyll/Ms. Hyde: Start the date on the right foot

A friend told me how his last date lasted 5 minutes. He's an affable, considerate, tolerant guy, so I couldn't imagine what could go wrong in 5 minutes.

He said he'd had great, fun, pleasant, in-depth phone conversations with the woman, then asked her to a high-end restaurant for dinner. Nearly immediately after sitting down, she started telling him he was too religious and finding fault with other aspects of his life that are important to him. Even for this patient, sweet guy, enough was enough. He said "This isn't working for me," paid for the wine and left. He

> *She started finding fault with aspects of his life that are important to him*

said he'd felt he had met Dr. Jekyll and Ms. Hyde.

If she had trouble with his religiousness, she should not have accepted the date. Telling him was not going to change him. The only thing it changed was his willingness to stick around and treat her to a nice evening.

First dates are about getting to know each other, not about fault-finding. You should be your best self — being on your best behavior but being yourself as well. You shouldn't pretend you are someone you aren't, but you should work to make yourself appealing enough that he wants to see you again.

# *One-date wonders*

ou know how some music artists are called "one-hit wonders" because they had one hit song and never again appeared on the Billboard charts? I have my dating version of that — one-date wonders. These are guys who after one date were at the top of *my* chart, but we didn't see each other again.

Luckily, it hasn't happened very often — so far, only three times. I've been attracted to him, but either the attraction wasn't returned or something else happened. Here's my countdown.

- In the #3 spot is the tall, blonde, green-eyed sales executive who was enlightened, funny, and spiritual. The lunch date passed quickly as our discussion topics never ended. And they were interesting topics, not just the usual personal history. But alas, he wrote an email afterwards saying that we were not a match and could we be friends. I responded "Of course. I'd love to stay in contact." I never heard from him again.

- Number 2 is the tall, fun, former Navy Seal, chief financial officer (See "Dear Fido" in the *Winning at the Online Dating Game: Stack the Deck in Your Favor* book.). We had fun, witty emails and calls and a two-hour coffee. I thought we hit it off, but once again I misread his attentiveness, as I never heard from him again.

And topping the chart is the sexy, cute, tall, affectionate airline pilot with the fantastic sense of humor and the deep, resonant voice. I was smitten during our three-hour coffee date, and we were holding hands within an hour. I couldn't wait for the good-night kiss, and it was as fantastic as the rest of him. He called the next day to set up a dinner date a few days later. I was so excited, I planned my outfit based on what I knew he liked.

The morning of the date he called to say he needed to cancel as he had begun dating another woman before me (we both shared we were dating around in our quest of "the one") and thought he could juggle two women, but saw he couldn't. He didn't think it would be fair to either of us. While I was disappointed, I thought he had courage to call me — not email me — and discuss it with me. I occasionally send him "hi" emails just in case it doesn't work out with her! But after a year, his most recent email said they are still together.

# *Do you hide your "light" from a date?*

A gal pal asked me, "How do your dates react when they learn of your accomplishments?"

I responded, "Most don't know about them."

"Really? Why not?"

"Because I don't tell them."

"Why?"

"First of all, it's not like I'm a Nobel laureate, Supreme Court judge, Academy Award nominee or brain surgeon. My accomplishments pale compared to other people I know.

"Secondly, some men are intimidated by my resume, even though I know others who have a much more impressive one. I don't want to start out with someone being threatened. So I don't bring up anything I think would be intimidating — at least generally not on the first date.

"Thirdly, I find it off-putting when a guy recites his resume on the first date. It's okay if something comes up in context of the conversation, like, 'I got used to feeling stupid when I felt I was the dumbest Rhodes scholar that year' or 'When I was at Harvard, they had these silly hazings.'"

"And fourth, some people would think I'm rich based on what they read on my web site. I'm not. I don't want a gold digger."

"But you're hiding your light under a bushel."

She's right. I hide a bit of who I am at first. I am not meaning to be dishonest, but I dole out parts of who I am — including warts — as I get to know someone. I need to trust that he likes me for my personality, not only for my accomplishments. Of course I could argue that these make up a big part of who I am.

> *I dole out parts of who I am as I get to know someone.*

Rocket Man (described in the *In Search of King Charming: Who Do I Want to Share My Throne?* book) said he was at first intimidated by my web page listing of accomplishments. This from an Academy Award-winning special-effects producer who's called a legend in the industry. He's intimidated by me? We identify ourselves at some level by our achievements, even if we don't flaunt them.

So if your accomplishments are integral to who you are, why hide them? I think we don't want to drive someone away. We don't want to seem that we are boasting. And we don't want to be perceived as way beyond the other's status. The truth is, achievements don't always translate into economic assets. In fact, some say there is an "Oscar curse" where recipients have trouble getting work after winning, as others think they are too expensive for their projects.

Do you hide your "light" — your accomplishments — from dates? If so, when do you let out shafts of your light for him to see? If you do hide some of your light, why?

# *Love me tender*

The lyrics in Elvis' song say it succinctly: Love me tenderly and sweetly. And when you do, I don't want you ever to let me go. I want that tenderness and sweetness to last forever.

The dictionary defines tender as "showing gentleness and concern or sympathy; loving kindness, kindheartedness, compassion, care, benevolence."

We want someone to love us tenderly, who will treat us with care and kindness. We want to be spoken to and treated with thoughtfulness and concern, with some sensitivity for how the words might land in our ears.

That's not to say we aren't willing to hear things we don't want to hear. While some prefer truth without a cushion, I and other women want honesty wrapped in a soft down comforter. We still want the truth, but we want it given to us softly, with care, concern and compassion.

This writing was prompted by a recent experience of my not feeling treated tenderly by a date. When I did something he didn't like, instead of telling me gently, it would come out brusquely. When I brought up something he didn't want to talk about, he said, "Don't go there," instead of "I'd rather we not discuss that right now." It was not only the pointed words, but the tone that made his comment feel harsh.

For example, reviewing the menu in a fish restaurant, he asked what sounded good to me. I listed several fish choices, then noticed a favorite dish. "And the smoked chicken risotto sounds good too."

"We're in a *fish* restaurant. You should have fish," was his response. I felt like a child being reprimanded by Dad. As an adult, aren't I allowed to have whatever I want without a "should" attached or my choice being questioned? Of course.

> I felt like a child being reprimanded by Dad

When he groped me in public, I said I was uncomfortable and requested he not do it again. While I knew he was trying to be playful, it felt disrespectful. Instead of listening or apologizing, he said, "No one saw. And if they did, what do I care what they think? And you shouldn't care what they think." Thus he negated my feelings. He showed he didn't care how I thought or felt.

Other comments accumulated that were small affronts. Nothing major, so I thought I wouldn't make a big deal about them. We were just getting to know each other, so why continually be nitpicking minor infractions? While he showed tenderness in other ways, I was feeling less and less cared for. I don't want to feel verbal pinpricks throughout an evening.

I'm sure if I'd told him I didn't feel he was being tender he would be incredulous. He was tender in his focus on me, physically with the exception of the incident above, and his general conversation. He had no idea how his comments were coming across, as when I did say something, he got defensive. In his 20-year marriage and subsequent relationships had no one given him this feedback? I'd guess no. Based on his descriptions of his past, I don't think those women were any more astute about this than he.

What do you think about tenderness? Is that a requirement in your romantic relationship? Are you as sensitive to this as I am, or do you have thicker skin?

# "When can I meet your kids?"

I have never asked a guy this. However, a woman recently shared that she asks this on the first date. Additionally she asks, "When would you be comfortable meeting mine, and each others' friends?"

Even though I don't have kids, I know how protective most people are of theirs and of introducing them to people they're dating. Most don't want to parade a bunch of dates by their kids, but instead want to only introduce them to each other after dating someone for a while.

My pal feels differently. She says her teenaged daughter is comfortable meeting her dates early on, and she knows a man cares about her if he introduces his kids to her. If a man balks or says it will take 6 months, she

> *He knows a man cares about her if he introduces his kids to her*

doesn't see him again. She says that's just too long. It limits when they can see each other to when he doesn't have his kids.

Since this isn't an issue for me, I asked some dating moms what they thought. Most agreed that asking about when to meet the kids was not an appropriate first-date question. The consensus was also that kid meeting generally happens after a few months of exclusive dating.

I don't ask to meet the kids — even if they are grown. I figure a man knows when he wants this to happen and will bring it up when he does. I'm not in a hurry so I let it evolve organically.

If you have kids, how long do you need to date someone before you introduce them to each other? If you don't have children, when would you expect to be introduced? Do you ask to meet his kids?

# When do you tell your date about irritants?

There seem to be several camps on this:

1.  Immediately when the annoyance happens, even on the first date. Say something so he can modify his behavior. No matter how small the irritation, you should say something when it happens.

2.  Not on the first date, unless the behavior is egregious (blowing his nose in the cloth napkin, walking 5 paces in front of you, wearing a hat inside a nice restaurant, fondling you in public).

3.  Only when it happens frequently enough that you can't tolerate it anymore. Giving someone grace shows maturity unless you can't stand that pen-top clicking, fingernail-tooth cleaning, or utterance of "cool," "like," or "ya know" one more time.

4.  Only if you think you're interested in seeing him in the future. Why bring it up if you have no interest in him?

My preference is a combination of 2, 3 and 4. When I've had dates who subscribe to #1 and nit pick about what I consider minor infractions, the cumulative effect is I feel picked on.

This is something that I wouldn't have thought to be a deal breaker. But it has been. More than once.

Here are some things to ponder about feedback:

*Frequency.* It's not just what someone nitpicks about. It's the frequency. If he brings to my attention every detail he doesn't like, it gets trying. You need to pick your battles and only point out behaviors you find obnoxious. So when he wipes clean his silverware in an upscale restaurant, notice his anal retentiveness, but don't comment. Unless he starts doing it for the couple at the next table.

*Tone.* Someone's tone is important as well. I can take constructive feedback, but not easily if someone has an irritated tone or sounds as if I'm an idiot for behaving a certain way. I try to have a patient tone, but I know that when you let an irritant go on too long, it does come through in your "that's the last straw" voice.

*Phrasing.* How the feedback is phrased is important, too. Some people like you to blurt out the problem, "You have bad breath," vs. a softer, more indirect choice, "Let's have a mint before we continue kissing." Men tell me the latter drives them crazy, yet many women find the former too blunt and insensitive. Ah, the differences in the genders!

💜 *Location.* The place is important, too. Don't criticize a man in front of others. If he's doing something you find offensive, either whisper it to him, or get him to step away from the others. He can become embarrassed — as would you — to hear it in front of friends or colleagues. Also, bringing something up over a nice, romantic dinner can ruin the evening. If it can wait, leave it for later.

💜 *Balance with positives.* I heard a suggestion that for every one piece of corrective feedback, you should have 5 positives. Otherwise the receiver will feel as I did, continually nagged.

I went out several times with a man who had rigid expectations on when I should bring up anything that bothered me. During our time together, if I did anything he didn't like, he told me immediately. I, on the other hand, let most things go, giving him grace. However, not saying something about his nitpicking resulted in my feeling continually criticized.

When I explained I had a different philosophy about when to deliver corrective communication, he said, "You have to say something at the time. You can't say something hours later. It's wrong. If you don't say something at the time, you shouldn't bring it up later."

His rule was, if you didn't bring it up instantly upon happening, you abdicated your right to bring it up ever. I reminded him, "We talked about this on the phone. I told you I often brought up things as they happen, but sometimes I don't realize how I feel about something until a little later."

"No, you have to bring it up at the time." Now I saw that he had no concept that one could experience a feeling, like a mild irritation, but be unable to articulate why until a little later. In his mind, everyone must say what was bothersome at the moment or relinquish the chance to discuss it later. Trying to explain this concept was futile, like trying to explain a beautiful sunset to a blind person.

I realized I couldn't be with someone who had such rigid rules about what was "right" behavior from their partner, especially behavior I couldn't control. I needed someone who could listen and gently probe if I was upset, not get angry and defensive, just as I would him. While I enjoyed many things about him, I saw that he didn't have the communication skills I find essential for a long-term romantic partner. Needless to say, we didn't see each other again.

Which camp(s) are you in?

# *Honesty is not always the best policy*

No, I am not suggesting you lie. I am suggesting, however, that there are times when full honesty is not the best at the time.

For example, full disclosure is not always necessary on a first date. Guys have told me they were still living with their estranged wives, had been adulterers, were being sued by their ex-girlfriend, had an IRS lien on their house, had done something illegal, and had an STD. A doctor date disclosed his license had been on probation for carrying a concealed weapon and brought the paperwork to show the probation was complete. Another shared his ex had called the cops accusing him of child molesta-

*Full disclosure is not always necessary on a first date*

tion. And one man explained he enjoyed dressing in women's clothes!

Now all of these things would be important to know — if I was interested in going further. However, I think it would have been fine if I was told on the second date. I'm sure the guys thought they were being forthright — which they were — by disclosing possible deal breakers from the beginning. I just thought this sort of total honesty was a bit much for a first "let's meet" date. In fact, most of these disclosures meant there was not a second date, so you could say they saved me time and energy.

Another time full honesty may not be the best policy is when you are saying you don't want to see him again. You could list the litany of his character flaws to show why you aren't a good match. However, a dear friend was recently devastated when a woman he dated a few times told him she didn't want to see him again because he was too effeminate. He knew he was a "soft" man, so this did nothing to help him and affected his self-esteem thinking no woman would find him attractive.

So disclose what you think might be a deal breaker, but hold some things in reserve for the second date. Some things you think might be a deal breaker actually won't be for the right guy.

# Men behaving badly

I rarely talk about "bad" dates, because if a date doesn't work out, it just wasn't meant to be. No use lingering on what didn't work or what an unpleasant experience it was.

When people hear I've written a series of books about midlife dating many immediately say, "I should write a book about all the bad dates I've had." Generally, I don't think people want to hear about bad dates, unless they are out of the dating scene. Then the stories can be funny, but are usually sad.

I think most of us want to hear about the good dates, which gives us hope that there are great singles out there, not mashers, players and cads. However, the reality is, there are some not-so-great people in the singles scene.

A friend theorizes that part of the reason we come across some of these folks is because it's so much easier for someone to enter the dating scene via online dating. You don't even have to pay to post a profile on most sites. So people who would not date in the "real" world — meeting people in classes, at work, at shared hobbies, at friends' houses, at bars — are in the dating pool because it's easy. So the pool has gotten a tad polluted, and we encounter folks we might not have before.

In fact, I read that a third of those listed on online dating sites haven't met anyone in person as a result of their online activities. So would those third be considered "dating" if they weren't listed online? I don't think so. Nearly half have met 1 to 5 others. What the report didn't say was in what time period — a month, 6 months, year, more than a year?

Out of the 112 men I've gone out with I can think of only a few "bad" first dates. Compared to other stories I've heard about bad first dates, these are pretty tame. Most "bad" dates just aren't a good fit, here are the recaps of the nine, and even some of them weren't really "bad," just not a fit:

❤ ***Too-Much-Too-Fast Guy*** — We'd talked for a week on the phone and email. We decided to meet for a drink at a nearby karaoke bar. When I arrived at the darkened bar, he looked little like his picture, but he recognized me. As I slid into the booth, he leaned over and kissed me on the lips. A tad forward, but I let it slide. We talked. He reached over and took my hand. More talking. He asked if I wanted to dance. I did. He held me close. When we came back to the booth, he slid closer to me. He pulled me toward him for another kiss. Then another. Soon he was French kissing me. I said it was too much for a public place. He said, "You said you liked public displays of affection!" "Yes, but this is too soon." I slid away from him and said I needed to be going.

💜 *The Masher.* We'd flirted with daily emails for nearly a month since I was out of the country and we couldn't meet before then. When we did meet in a pub, his greeting was a French kiss! I said that was a bit too much too soon, and he shrugged it off. We went to a nearby table where he sat next to me. He continued to kiss me while we sipped wine. Finally, I said I was hungry so we went next door to have dinner. As soon as we sat down, he said, "I live nearby. Let's go to my house." No, that won't be happening.

💜 *10-Minute Guy* — We'd met mid-afternoon at a shopping mall. The plan was to do a little shopping, have dinner, then either see a movie or go dancing. Within 10 minutes he said, "I'm going to go." I asked if he was feeling okay. He said, "Yes. I'm just not attracted." My jaw dropped as he turned and left.

💜 *The Vexing Vietnam Vet* — He had been a tad demanding on the phone, but I thought I'd give him a chance, so I accepted a drink invitation. In an empty tavern we had soft drinks and an appetizer while he told me grisly story after story of his days in Vietnam. When I tried to change the subject, he came back with other stories of his heroism, always heavily laced with expletives. He reached across the table and took my hand. When he asked if we should do this again, I was taken aback, so stammered, "That would be interesting." No, we won't be doing it again.

💚 ***The Obnoxious Ophthalmologist*** — Ironically, he's one of the few men who I didn't recognize from his photos, yet he complained about women posting 10-year-old or 80-pounds-ago pics. He said we'd meet at the restaurant, which I thought meant at the reception area. He was in the bar and I waited 10 minutes before checking to see if he might be there. He was barely cordial from the moment I sat down and made no effort to get the waiter to take my drink order. His demeanor shouted that he was not at all interested in me and could we make this as short as possible. To add insult to injury, he sent a snotty email afterwards. Obviously this doctor had no bedside manner.

💚 ***Mr. Aggressive*** — He was cuter than his picture. We chatted at the coffee shop, then he asked if I wanted to have dinner. I did. When we walked to find a restaurant, he turned and kissed me. A bit soon, but I was flattered at the same time taken aback. After dinner, I mentioned I liked CSI and it was on that night. He said, "I own a home nearby that is being renovated. Let's go watch it there." When I declined, he was insistent, not relenting in his nearly demanding we go there. No, I wouldn't be going to this guy's house on the first — nor any — date.

💚 ***The Uneducated College Grad*** — I wrote about him in "Date turns out to be losing bet" (page 35). I should have known from his calls and emails that he wasn't for me. But I let my self-interest overcome my instinct. His emails and conversation were laced with bad grammar, poor spelling, incorrect word usage, poor pronunciation. When he told me his alma mater, I thought, "If I were the Admissions Office, I'd ban him from telling anyone he'd graduated here." I understood why he still lived with his mother at age 41.

*The Overly "Cool" Dude* — He was sweet, smart and complimentary on the daily calls and in flirty emails. He said he was very interested in me and hoped it worked out for us, as he could see a future together. When we met, he spent 80% of the time talking about himself, and when I tried to interject, he said, "I'm going to cut you off" and continued to talk about himself. At the white-tablecloth restaurant, he brought his own cheap wine so he wouldn't have to pay $20 for the $5 bottle. He ate his lamb chops with his hands. Every fifth word was "cool." He French kissed me within moments of our meeting. No, we will not be having a future together.

*The Revolting Ravager* — His greeting me by groping my tush said it all in seconds. But I was too overwhelmed with incredulousness to throw my drink in his face. I stayed longer than was warranted, but I just couldn't believe what was coming out of this man's mouth. It was like interacting with someone from another culture — or planet! How could he possibly think that he was being alluring with talk of taking me out to my car and ravishing me? See "Lessons from a bad date" (page 67) for the whole story.

Can you avoid bad first dates? I think you can reduce the possibility considerably by having some email and phone conversations for a few days to a week. If the conversation turns to sex before you've even met, then don't meet him. If he shows he has opposite values than you, don't bother. There are a number of men I've had phone or email conversations with that I then didn't meet. Not enough interest to invest the hour for coffee, plus time to get ready and drive to and from the coffee shop.

So don't be afraid of bad first dates. They happen. My experience is about 10% of the dates fall into this category. Not bad, really. So expect there will be some misses, but don't linger on them. And don't share them with your next date, as he'll wonder what kind of story you'll tell about him afterwards!

# Chemistry, or does he make my toes curl?

Chemistry is often listed as what one wants in a relationship. However no one can seem to describe what that is. They just say, "I'll know it when I feel it."

*"I'll know it when I feel it."*

It is attraction. For men it seems to be "I want to be intimate with this person." For women, it can be "I feel great around him. He makes me laugh, treats me the way I want to be treated, and seems to care about me." Women want to spend more time with the man. Men at least want to spend the night with the woman! And sometimes the same is true for the woman.

Since "chemistry" is nebulous and overused, I prefer the phrase "made my toes curl." Admittedly, it hasn't happened much, but when it does, you definitely know there is a connection.

However, I've found that sometimes the connection is just physical, and you can quickly be drawn into thinking that there is more. But after the physical is satisfied, you realize you don't have much connection with this person. So consider that if there is real chemistry and connection, it will still be there in a few weeks and months — and hopefully years, when by that time the lust may have passed.

After one date, a gentleman asked if I wanted to go out again. I said he was a great guy, but my toes didn't curl. While disappointed, he knew exactly what I meant.

# *Lessons from a bad date*

Once in a while, when you spin the dating wheel, it stops on "Bad Date." Of course you don't know this going into the date. And luckily, my experience is it only happens about 10% of the time. But this night I landed smack dab in the middle of that slot. Since it doesn't happen often, I wasn't prepared for it but still managed to eke out a few lessons. I'll tell you those after I set the scene.

We'd sent a handful of short emails and talked briefly on the phone a few times. His cell service was so bad, it dropped every third word, so I explained I couldn't hear him and we cut the calls short. Usually, I like to talk to a man a bit to know some about him before I agree to a meeting. Because of the bad phone coverage, I didn't know a lot about him going into our drink date.

I met him at a bar after a dinner meeting with colleagues. He waved as I entered. I wouldn't have recognized him from his picture, which I now saw was 20 years and 80 pounds ago. Still, I greeted him as I always do, with a brief hug. He didn't stand from the bar stool, but managed to slide a hand down to my tush. As I promptly removed it, I thought "Strike One."

This self-described "sophisticated, worldly and re-fined" man wore a well-worn suit jacket with an un-pressed shirt. He told me several times how he is the sole heir to a local mega-business so was very wealthy. Funny, his tailor had yet to see any of this fortune.

When I sat down, his glass of champagne was half gone so I asked how long he'd been there. He'd just ar-rived. "And he'd already downed a half a glass?" I noted. I sipped mine as he began the interrogation.

When I tried to reply to his questions, he inter-rupted. Often he would tell me the same thing over and over and over again. He asked me to guess the answer to questions and when I did, of course it was wrong.

The conversation took a turn when he leaned to-ward me and said, "I want to take you out to your car and ravish you." He then continued with specifics of what this would entail. When I didn't respond by grab-bing him by the hand and rushing to the car, he decided he should increase the frequency of sharing his inten-tions, respited only briefly by non-sexual comments.

For example, when he learned I was born in Kansas, he decided to enlighten me on his opinion of Kansans: slow, stupid, uneducated, uncouth, unsophisticated, cautious, boring. When I failed to take him up on his offer for car sex, he began telling me how I was "so Kan-sas." Adding, "I mean no harm." Right. So in essence, I epitomized the adjectives he just used to describe Kan-sans. Charming.

He downed another glass of champagne while I was

halfway through my one.

We'd discovered on the phone that we'd concurrently attended the same university for two years, in fact, eating in the same cafeteria. When I brought up the college's name, he began to describe it as if I'd never been there.

He told me how he didn't like American women but loved European women. I wondered, "Then why don't you go live in Europe?" Probably because the women there would be no more enamored with him than we are.

Since I believe generally people have some treasure inside them if you are patient and willing to look, I worked hard to find something I liked about him. He was intelligent. Unfortunately, that was all I could find.

As he gulped his third glass of champagne in less than an hour, I decided I had given him enough time to see if it was worth investing any more. As I knew within the first few seconds, no. This was worth no more time, and I could have said so within the first 10 minutes. But I don't like it when someone cuts me off after so little time, so I wanted to see if it might improve. It didn't.

After Strike One I lost count. With baseball players the ones who hit the most home runs also strike out a lot. I don't think this man ever hit a home run, just had lots of strike outs.

What were my lessons?

💙 Stick with what has worked pretty well in the past — talk to the guy for more than a few minutes before agreeing to meet him.

💚 Continue with the "short first date" rule. In our phone calls, he'd asked more than once to have dinner with him. I can imagine how excruciating that would have been.

💚 If his picture is from a previous decade, he doesn't understand that truth in advertising is key to dating ethically.

💚 If he does something egregious at the beginning, it's not going to get any better. He's clueless how to treat a woman respectfully.

💚 If he talks graphically about sex, leave.

💚 If he repeats himself frequently, he's not present.

💚 If he downs three drinks within an hour, he's probably an alcoholic. Leave when you notice two are downed in a half an hour.

💚 Appreciate the "normal" guys, who are gentlemanly, kind and can keep the conversation out of the gutter.

What have you learned when the dating wheel has landed on "Bad Date"?

# *Do you get his motor running, or why does he read "easy" on your forehead?*

A male friend was analyzing why the majority of the "bad" dates listed in "Men behaving badly" (page 59) involved men moving too fast. We discussed if these guys were just horn dogs or if I was sending off subtle signals that were being misinterpreted.

**He:** How do you behave in pre-meeting phone calls and emails?

**DG:** I'm flirty, but not sexual. I compliment him on things he says or has accomplished. I ask questions, contribute to the conversation, and laugh appropriately. I am not suggestive or sexual.

**He:** How do you behave on a first date?

**DG:** I'm focused, pay attention to my date, smile, laugh, and if I like him, I might touch his arm. If I feel a warm connection to him from multiple emails and calls, I'd give him a hug hello.

However, I don't initiate hand holding or kissing. And I certainly don't start sexual conversations. And if he starts one, I work to keep it tame.

**He:** I think because you are warm, playful and flirty in emails and calls, when the guy meets you his motor is already running.

This means the guy is already feeling sexual toward me. He may have entertained fantasies (some have shared they have). Then when he meets me, if he likes what he sees, he goes into behavior that would usually be reserved for later dates. Because we have already bonded to some degree beforehand, it feels like we already know each other, so the first meeting is somewhat a formality.

Thus he feels comfortable going for a passionate kiss or other signs of affection. In his mind, we are already on a second or third date since we know a bit about each other and already like each other.

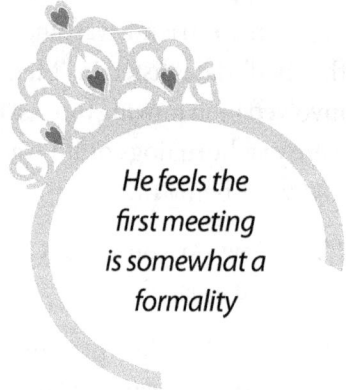

*He feels the first meeting is somewhat a formality*

So, while I felt these guys were treating me as if I had

"slut" written on my forehead, they were just responding to the warm connection they were feeling. Smiling and steady eye contact is interpreted as interest, so since I am comfortable doing both, the guy was seeing green lights everywhere. Coupled with some touching, he thought I was inviting him to move full speed ahead.

So what to do to slow a guy down? Do I have to change my personality and demeanor entirely? I don't want to give off false signals, but I also don't want to be someone who acts cold or disinterested, doesn't smile or breaks eye contact when I like a guy. Now I am better at saying, "We need to slow down," when he's coming on like a locomotive. If he doesn't back off, then time to extricate myself.

What signals do you think you send that are misinterpreted? How do you slow down overeager guys that doesn't involve a glass of ice water to overheated body parts?

# A favorite question to ask

**D**r. Phil says we don't ask the right questions when determining if someone might be a good match for us. I'm sure he's right. I now have a list of questions I wish I'd asked.

One of my favorite questions to ask tells me a lot about the man. I explain that I was invited to a Halloween singles' dance. The invitation said to come dressed as "your shadow side" — the part of you you're not proud others know about you. Things like you're a slob, couch potato, controlling, etc. I pondered dressing in several costumes, like a judge's robe because my ex said I was judgmental, or a witch with a big "B" on my chest because... well you know why. Before I tell him what I finally decided on, I ask what costumes he'd consider.

> I ask what costumes he'd consider

His response tells me a lot. If he can't think of anything he's not proud of, it tells me he's not very introspective. We all have things we want to change. If he comes up with things like "Superman," he's not clear on the concept of "shadow side."

Even if he doesn't come up with something immediately, his reaction to the question and discussion around this tell me a lot.

What question could you ask that tells you a lot?

# Women's first-date blunders

n "First-date red flags that this guy isn't for you" (page 29) I talked about what men do that tell you they should be released back into the dating pool. I've been curious what women do that make a man say, "She's not for me." Of course, everyone has their individual deal breakers, so I interviewed a few single guy pals to see if there were some common behaviors that drove them batty. Here's what I gleaned.

💗 *Telling your date you've talked about him to your mother.* It assumes too much permanency before even meeting. He'll assume you want to marry him as quickly as possible. "You can hear the bear trap starting to close," said one friend.

💗 *Sharing your baggage.* Women disclose too much too soon. Save it for the second or subsequent dates. If you share too much on the first date, he'll question your judgment about how much you tell a stranger in any situation. Hold on to see if there's enough interest for a second date, then you can begin to slowly let your baggage come out.

💜 ***Telling him your marriage time line.*** You tell him you want to be married within a year — on the first date? Watch this man run from the building.

💜 ***Coming on too strong sexually.*** Some women talk about sex or are too aggressive and physical on the first date, kissing, rubbing and trying to seduce a man who isn't interested in being seduced — at least not at a first meeting. Of course, a few like it!

💜 ***Nitpicking his values, life style or behaviors.*** If you don't like something, decide if you can live with it or suggest changing it later, not the first date! If you can't live with it, don't accept a second date.

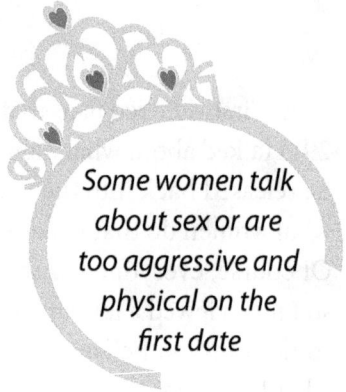

> *Some women talk about sex or are too aggressive and physical on the first date*

💜 ***Bashing men.*** It seems both genders like to tell stories about their exes or bad dates. However, if you say things like, "All men want is sex," or "Men are such jerks" you are lumping your date in with the others who've wronged you. No one likes to be stereotyped without a chance to show he's not like the others.

💚 ***Primping at the table.*** Some men despise when a woman freshens her makeup at the table or brushes her hair in a public place. Excuse yourself to the ladies room.

💚 ***Ordering expensive dishes then not eating them.*** Women have the rap of constantly being on a diet so they pick at their food. It irritates guys when a woman orders an appetizer, salad and lobster and only eats a little of each. If you know you are a light eater, offer to share something with him. Only order what you can realistically make a dent in. He's also not fond of your taking home a doggie bag, as he feels he's underwriting your next meal.

💚 ***Drinking too much.*** No one likes to be around someone who's sloshed. Limit your alcohol consumption to one or two.

💚 ***Talking incessantly or loudly.*** Some women (and some men, too) are afraid of dead air. A pause once in a while is a good thing, as is asking him questions about his opinions and life, as long as you don't interrogate him. Also, men complain that some women don't know how to keep their voices down, and the increased volume comes across shrill.

# Dating as a job interview

Early on, I scoffed when I was told men see dating as a job interview. How could finding love be similar to finding a job?

But then a 45-year-old man recited his resume to me. I learned where and when he went to school, his major, and a listing of his jobs, including dates and companies.

*A 45-year-old man recited his resume to me*

Since then I see the job interview parallel is more on target than I originally thought. I am dismayed when a potential suitor has not reviewed my profile before calling or meeting, so asks me things I've been clear about in my profile. As an employer, I would not be keen on someone who shows up for a job interview without reviewing the ad or job description.

If he shows up late or unkempt, I am also not impressed. If he talks too much about what he wants without asking what I want, or ignores my offering what I'm looking for, then we aren't a fit. Just like a job interview, there needs to be give and take on what is needed to be a good match.

I wonder if men would approach their next job interview with the same cavalierness that they do dating? If so, I can understand why some stay single for so long.

For a recent date I visited his web site, read his bio, and printed his profile. I reviewed it before I left home so I could be conversant on important things in his life.

# Go dutch or accept your date's offer to treat?

I was talking to a gal pal about how to deal with paying for a meal when you're first dating someone.

**Friend:** I always insist on paying for my own meal. At least until we're going together exclusively.

**DG:** Why do you insist?

**Friend:** I don't want to feel beholden.

**DG:** Beholden for what?

**Friend:** I don't want him to think I owe him sex for treating me to dinner.

**DG:** I don't think many men would think they are buying sex for the price of a dinner. Unless they're taking out a call girl!

**Friend:** I know. You're right.

**DG:** So what happens when the check comes?

**Friend:** As soon as the server puts it on the table I say,

"Let's split it."

*DG:* What if your date says, "Please allow me to get this."

*Friend:* I say, "No, I want to split it."

*DG:* Why is it important to you to go dutch?

*Friend:* I just feel guilty if my date pays.

*DG:* Why do you feel guilty?

*Friend:* I don't want him to think I'm cheap.

*DG:* What if he gave you a present. Would you accept it graciously?

*Friend:* Yes, if it wasn't something really expensive.

*DG:* Would you feel beholden or guilty?

*Friend:* No.

*DG:* Can you see that his wanting to treat you is similar to him wanting to give you a present. The present is a nice meal and he wants to treat you because he enjoyed your company. When you don't accept his gift, you are saying, "No, I don't want to receive anything from you." It puts up a barrier. It's a control issue. You're not allowing him to feel good about doing something for you and for which he's received enjoyment, too.

*Friend:* When you put it that way, it makes sense. But then I'd want to pay for after-dinner drinks. Or I'd say, "Next time it's on me." That will guarantee a second date!

**DG:** That's fine, if that's what you want. However, if he isn't interested in you, promising to pay for dinner next time isn't going to get him to want to spend another evening with you.

So on your date tonight, when the check comes and he says he'd like to treat, what will you say?

**Friend:** I'll say, "Thank you. That is generous of you. It was a great meal. I'd like to treat us to a nightcap."

It is fine to go dutch on early dates if you want. It's even okay to let the guy know this when you accept his invitation. And it's also acceptable to take turns treating. My ex and I did this when we first dated, as neither of us made much money then.

*Go dutch on early dates if you want*

However, my experience is that most midlife men will expect, and — most of the time — want to treat on the first date or two. This is why you should always let him choose the place you meet. If he isn't from the area and asks you to pick, give him descriptions of three restaurants that aren't the most expensive in town, unless he says he wants to try some top-of-the-line hot spots in your area.

If nothing has been said ahead of time, when the check comes don't excuse yourself to the rest room.

Men hate that. And don't let it just sit there for a long, long time.

When the check comes, if he grabs it and pulls out his wallet, that signals he wants and expects to pay. If the check sits there for a minute or two, I find the best way to handle it on a first date is to reach for my wallet and say, "How would you like to handle this?" I don't physically pick up the check or tray. I just reach for or pull out my wallet and ask the question. Nine times out of 10, the man will say, "I've got it," or "Allow me." If he's had a nice time, he'll gladly spring for lunch or dinner, even if he doesn't plan to ask you out again.

At that point, don't argue with him or snatch the check away and say, "My treat." Most men feel this is emasculating. Even if you make more money than he, don't do this.

*"How would you like to handle this?"*

I know some women have different experiences on this, but mine is that if a man accepts your splitting the bill, assuming you haven't ordered a much more expensive meal and/or drinks than him, he won't ask for a second date.

My ex and I shared all entertainment costs during our 20 years together. Occasionally, when one of us closed a big deal or for the other's birthday, we'd treat

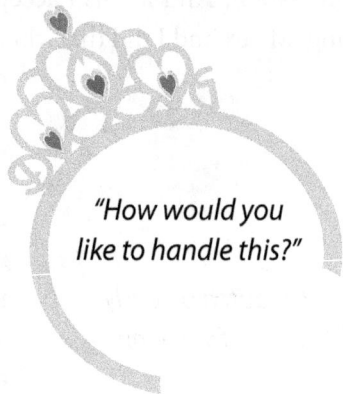

the other. But generally, we split it all. It was hard for me when first dating to feel okay about not sharing the cost, nor insist on taking turns. John Gray and others helped me see that this is not what most midlife men want, no matter how progressive they are — at least at first. Not all, but many, many men see picking up the check as part of his romancing you. When you insist on reciprocating tit for tat, it diminishes the positive feeling he gets by taking you out.

To even things out, if you can cook, ask him over for a special meal. If you can't cook, invite him over and bring in some food from a great restaurant. How is that different than treating him in a restaurant? I know, it's pretty comparable. But somehow, hosting someone at your home has more of a special feel to it.

How do you feel about splitting the check the first few dates?

# Do you like who you're being when with your date?

People often use the phrase, "He made me feel (bad, stupid, ugly, fat, angry, good, sexy, pretty)." The truth is, no one makes you feel anything. You choose to feel that way. Eleanor Roosevelt said, "No one makes you feel inferior without your consent." And that goes for any other emotion.

However, you can react to someone in a way that you don't like. He triggers something in you and you then respond a certain way — a way you don't like. It is still a choice of how to behave, but sometime he sparks something so ingrained in you it doesn't feel like you have a choice.

One of the checks for whether I want to be with a guy is how I behave around him. Do I like how I'm being? Or does he elicit behavior in me I don't like —

bitchiness, judgmental, pettiness, anger, irritation, manipulation. If I don't like how I'm being, of course I can change. But that takes work. I want to be naturally giving, loving, caring, silly, relaxed, and honest. If these behaviors come easily, I know I want to spend more time with him. If I have to fight off the negative behaviors, he's probably not for me.

*If I have to fight off my negative behaviors, he's not for me*

Of course, negative triggers are sometimes good as they give you a chance to become aware of old patterns and internal tapes and work through the original wound. But if you're continually acting in ways you don't like or respect or aren't proud of, it's time to move on — and maybe get some counseling along the way to see why you'd attract and invite someone into your life who treats you in a way that you respond in ways you don't like and to heal that old wound.

But if you find yourself being the kind of person you want to be then keep him around. His behavior allows you to be your best in his presence.

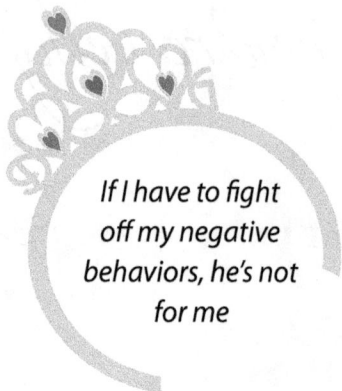

# *Help your date notice his riches*

> *"The greatest good you can do for another is not just to share your riches, but to reveal to him his own."*
> —Benjamin Disraeli

In the context of dating and relationships, I read this as being willing to share your skills and talents with your date without hiding any part of you. In "Do you hide your 'light' from a date?" (page 43) I shared how I have felt a need not to reveal many of my accomplishments with a date early on. By doing so, I'm hiding my "riches," as I've found many men — even accomplished ones — have been intimidated by my achievements. Disraeli is reminding us that part of our greatest good is not to leave part of who you are at the door.

I find the second part of the quote interesting and true, too. Many people are so used to their own talents that they discount them when pointed out. Part of this is society's frowning on pridefulness and boastfulness. And part of it is that when someone is good at something that comes naturally, or something they mastered a long time ago, they take it for granted. Friends who are concert-level musicians are modest about their skills. Excellent writer or speaker colleagues are humble when receiving accolades.

When you help your date see where he excels, especially if it something that he doesn't even notice, it reminds him of his special gifts. Once he is able to fully appreciate your sincere acknowledgment, it helps him own it himself. He may stand a bit straighter, have more spring in his step, or show a broader smile.

It is easy to point out someone's shortcomings. But it takes an aware person to first notice someone's "riches" of character, spirit, or talent. Then it takes a special skill to go beyond noticing and sincerely express your awe without fawning.

> *"Kind words can be short and easy to speak, but their echoes are truly endless."* —Mother Teresa

Anytime you notice a date's riches (not monetary), tell him what you see. Even if there is not a second date, your kind words will echo for him longer than you can imagine.

# "Tell me about yourself"

The first real-time contact with a potential date can be awkward. You may have a sketchy description from an online profile, or just a few minutes of information from the friend who connected you. You want to find out more about him, but you're not sure how to ask without seeming like you're interrogating. So how do you ask?

There are many ways. But let's start with a question that gets the hairs on my neck standing on end. It is the seemingly innocuous:

"Tell me about yourself."

Why does this irritate me so? Because it is so brainless. It says, "I haven't bothered to read or remember anything about you from your online profile, emails or phone connversation. So instead of asking you to tell me more detail about what I know about you, I'm asking the most inane question I can muster. I'm not very creative, thoughtful, or inquisitive."

Equally inane ones are,

"Why are you still single?"

"Why did you divorce?"

"Do you have kids?" (It says I don't in my profile. You read my profile, right? I didn't think so.)

"Why haven't you married?" (To someone who says he's not divorced or separated.)

Here are some ones I've found more interesting:

"What's your favorite response to 'Why are you still single?'"

"What do you feel you might have done to save your marriage?"

"What's your favorite part about being a dad?"

"In your next relationship, how do you want to prevent whatever went awry in your marriage?"

There are myriad other questions you can ask which get progressively deeper and more revealing as you get to know him. The point is before you speak to him, think about some gently probing questions you can ask. Don't be confrontational, but ask questions that get you to uncover values you find important.

*Think about some gently probing questions you can ask*

Once I went out with a man who complained that his divorce cost him over $100,000, even though he told me the

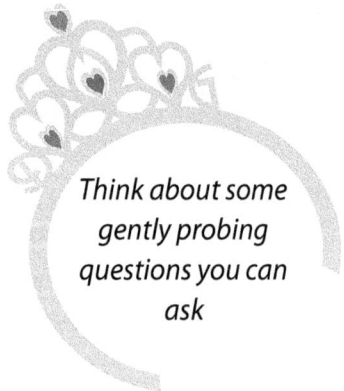

marriage was over years before and they just stayed to-gether for the kids. I asked, "If it was over long ago for both of you, why was she so acrimonious?" He paused for a moment, as apparently no one had ever asked that before. Then he said, "Probably because of my extra-marital relationships." I said, "Yes, that would do it!"

You can learn a lot not only by what a person asks you, but how he answers your questions. Try to make yours interesting, unusual and about issues that are im-portant to you.

# You can tell in the first 30 minutes

When I first started dating, a family-counselor friend told me that I'd know all I need to know if a man is a fit for me within the first 30 minutes of meeting him. I was incredulous.

*"Within only 30 minutes I will know if he is a fit for me? Not a full date?"*

*"No, you won't need longer," she responded. "You will be able to tell what you need to know within less than an hour. If you want to give him a full evening, that's fine, but I think you'll know pretty quickly."*

I've thought about this as I've been dating. Was she right? Could I tell if I wanted to know someone better and he'd be a good match for me within less than an hour?

The truth is, no, I haven't been able to tell if someone is a good match within the first hour. But I have known if a guy wasn't a match before the end of the first date. When I've decided to see him again, even though I knew we weren't a great match, it has ended, even though it may have taken 6 weeks to go through the process. Sometimes I thought I could overlook characteristics that meant we weren't a great match. But so far, of the men I've let go — vs. the men who've let me go — I could tell pretty quickly.

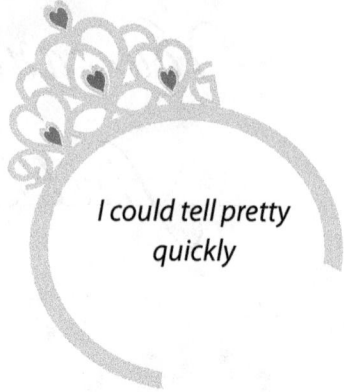

*I could tell pretty quickly*

So notice how you feel at the end of the first date and decide if you see enough of what you want in a mate to explore if you're a good match. If you're only seeing him again because you are lonely or bored or there's no one else on the horizon, do both of you a favor and don't accept a second date.

# *What do you think your date's car says about him?*

Some women judge a man by his car. If he drives an expensive car, she assumes he's financially sound. But he could be hocked up to his eyeballs to pay for it.

And men think a cool car equals sexiness. I met a potential suitor for coffee whose screen name was "Boxster." I watched him drive away — in his SUV. Maybe his Boxster was his other car — the one he drives when he wants to impress a date! Or maybe he chose that name hoping to entice women.

A man often poses next to his (or assumedly his) cool car and posts the pic on his online profile. One man showed himself next to a hot sports car. However, on closer inspection, the car was in a dealer's showroom! So either he had his pic taken while car shopping or he sold cars for a living.

A dating friend has two cars — a Toyota Echo and a convertible Mercedes Cabriolet. On a first date, he purposefully drives the Echo. He says if his date makes a negative comment or seems put off by his wheels, that's the last date.

For several months I dated a man who owned 5 cars — just for him. I joked that he could match his car to his outfit. But he drove the car that matched his mood. We most often went out in his Cadillac, sometimes the Oldsmobile, and only once in his $150,000 limited-edition Mercedes, which he saved mostly for driving to business meetings. But when alone, he most often drove the beat up Buick with ripped upholstery.

A gal pal told me her current beau owns nine cars.

What is it with men and cars? I've owned two cars at one time, but one was to be a gift to my niece when she turned 16. I understand that part of men's infatuation with cars has to do with phallic symbolism, especially for sports cars. And that a high-end car supposedly advertises success. And this car-equals-prowess goes back to high school when shallow girls thought a guy was hotter when he drove a cool car.

But evidentially midlife women are still impressed with some cars, and thus the men who drive them. I admit I notice if a man's car is clean and well kept. And yes, sporty cars are fun. Yet if a man isn't appealing, his car isn't going to turn that around. And if a man is alluring, it doesn't really matter what make or model he drives.

What do you think about what your date drives?

# Are you assessing — or judging — your date?

These terms are often used interchangeably. However, I see a difference.

Assessing is when you notice things about him. He's 6-feet tall, blue eyed, with dark curly hair. He has a little paunch, slouches, and interrupts often. He makes eye contact and speaks clearly.

Judging is when you put a value on what you see. He's tall — great! His eyes are beautiful, his hair luxuriant. His interrupting is annoying. He must have low self-esteem because he slouches. He's lazy, thus the paunch.

No one likes to be judged, but I'm afraid we frequently do it. We watch people in a coffee shop or an airport and go from noticing to judging in a nanosecond. The guy with the sour look on his face? He must be a grump. The woman with unkempt hair? Must not care about how she looks. The man with rippling muscles under his T-shirt? Must be a gym rat.

Assessing is just noticing, not making the assessment into judgment. You're like a tailor taking measurements without thinking, "This woman has fat thighs." He just notes the numbers without criticism.

How do you stay in assessing as long as possible with your date? You just note what you notice. You observe his physical appearance: height, weight, hair and eye color. You take in his clothing's style, fit and quality. You mentally note what he talks about, how he listens, the questions he asks, if he interrupts, how long he talks. You watch his body language, posture, facial expressions, eye contact, smile, how he sits and walks.

*The trick is to not make inferences without checking them out*

The trick is to not make inferences without checking them out. Let's take some of the examples from above:

- *The paunch* — He has been suffering from back and shoulder pain after a bike accident, so he has not been able to exercise for months. He's scheduled surgery soon, and he's looking forward to getting back in shape.

- *The slouch* — Because of his injury, it's painful to stand up straight. After his surgery, he'll be back into military form.

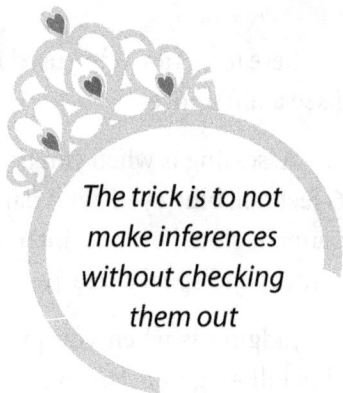

💜 ***Interrupting*** — His ex-wife talked non-stop and he found the only way he could get in the conversation was to interrupt her. She never said it bothered her, so it became a habit. He doesn't even realize he does it anymore.

Once you know more, the judgments don't hold. Ideally, put off deciding if you like or don't like a characteristic until you know the whole story. Just notice for now.

# *Stood up!*

ave you ever been stood up for a date? Whether you have already, or regrettably may be in the future, it's useful to examine your options. Here's how I explored mine.

A new potential suitor and I arranged for a dinner first date. He called two days beforehand to set a time. He asked me to choose a restaurant and email him the address. I did so within the hour, along with the restaurant's phone number and my cell number.

I got dated up and drove to the restaurant, arriving 10 minutes early. I waited. The appointed time came. He didn't waltz in. I gave him some grace, as he was driving from an hour away, so maybe he got caught in traffic. Another five minutes passed. Ten. I asked the hostess if she thought it rude, as I did, to be 10 minutes late and not call. When she found out where he was driving from, she thought he might have hit traffic. I called his cell phone to see if he was lost or stuck. Voice mail. I left a message.

Another five minutes passed. Then another. I called again. I didn't leave a message. I vacillated between fuming at his rudeness for not calling, worrying that something had happened which prevented him from calling, to wondering if I got the day wrong, or if he'd even received my email. I gave him a little more slack.

At 30 minutes after the time we set to meet, and 40 minutes after I arrived, I left. I called his cell one last time to see if I could get him, not his voice mail. I didn't leave a message.

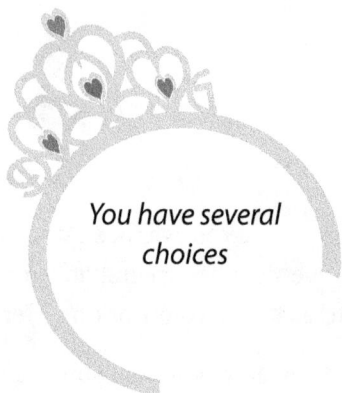

*You have several choices*

When this happens you have several choices:

- Should you call again? No. I left a message and he can see I called multiple times after that.

- Should you email to ask what happened? No.

- If he calls, how should you react? I'll be in wonder, curious at what happened. If he is contrite and apologetic and offers a plausible excuse — which needs to include the words "hospital" or "kidnapped" — I'll consider giving him another chance. But I can't imagine that his reason would be anything but inexcusable. I will let him know I was inconvenienced.

- If he doesn't call, oh well. Although he was charming on the phone and had a wonderful accent, deep voice and good sense of humor, he lives over an hour's drive from me, which is far from optimal. He's been married three times, and is only separated from his last wife, but they've filed for divorce. Orange flag (a mix of yellow and red flag.) He has a small child with her, which complicates life.

If he purposefully blew me off, what possibly could go through a man's mind to make this okay? Narcissism? Selfishness? Lack of compassion, empathy or humanity? If he decided not to meet me, what would prevent him from having the common decency to at least call and give me some feeble excuse, if not say he changed his mind or plans? As much as I want to be in wonder, this one has me flummoxed.

We'll see how this one plays out. I won't be waiting by my phone.

# When you're inappropriately dressed for a date

Y ou feel stupid. You forgot to ask about appropriate attire and just made an assumption. He'd invited you to dinner and you mistook the name of the restaurant for a high-end one with a similar name to this tavern. You're in a flirty, low-cut cocktail dress with glittering accessories and high heels, which is totally out of place for the shorts and t-shirts you see all other diners have donned. Your date is a tad dressier than they are, as he has on jeans and a long-sleeved shirt.

What to do?

First, acknowledge your faux pas to your date, as it will be obvious you misunderstood. Don't try to blame it on him for not telling you the appropriate dress. It's your responsibility to ask or to call the restaurant and inquire.

At this point you can't really change clothes or restaurants, as he's not appropriately dressed for a high-end place. If one of you lives nearby, you could suggest dashing home to change.

You can reduce the disconnect by removing some of your sparkles (bracelet, necklace, earrings), and/or letting down your hair if it's in a chignon.

Or you could laugh it off and have a great time. You will be the center of attention in this beer joint, so why not enjoy it?

*You could laugh it off and have a great time*

As a high-school senior, I was invited to join my best friend and her fiancé on a double date with his best friend. I'd met my date once and knew he was a few years older than me and had a good job. We would go to a nice restaurant for dinner, one I knew nothing about. I asked my friend what to wear.

*"Wear that dress you wore to your friend's college ball."*

*"The full-length gown?"*

*"Yes, that would be perfect."*

I spent the better part of the afternoon getting ready, putting my hair into a French twist and applying

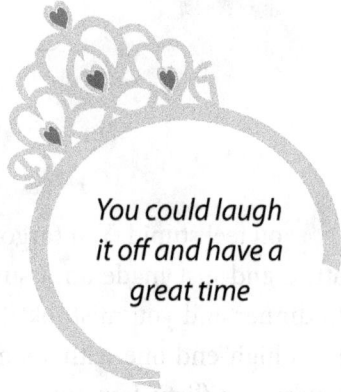

evening makeup to go with my floor-length prom dress. I was nervous as I hadn't dated much. So I didn't really know how to handle it when my date arrived at my door wearing a sports jacket and open-collared shirt.

I stuttered and stammered as I explained that this is what Gayle had told me to wear. I told him I'd go change, and he graciously said I looked great and I was fine as I was.

However, at the restaurant I observed that my friend was in a sundress and other diners were similarly attired. I tried to make the best of it and ignore being so out of place. As a seventeen-year-old I didn't have the wits to know how to dress down my gown even a bit.

I was mad at my friend for misguiding me. But I could have asked my date directly for the dress code. Which is what I do now when I have any doubt.

What would you do if you found yourself inappropriately dressed for a date?

# *What to wear to build rapport?*

My date was with an advertising agency owner who lives in a nearby laid-back resort town. We had a fun, interesting first conversation, and he asked me to join him for dinner at a midrange restaurant.

Now I must figure out what to wear.

I think women fret about this more than men. While some men may consciously choose to wear a shirt they've been told looks good on them or brings out their eyes, I think many don't give a lot of thought to what they'll wear on a first date. They may debate to don a sports coat or not, or take off a tie if coming from work.

But women seem to be more conscious of what messages they send off with what clothing. I don't mean to imply that a lot of women obsess about their attire, but I think most put some focus on what impression they want to give and which clothing will telegraph that message.

So I looked through my closet. I wanted to choose something that is fun and flirty, but not too revealing. I know cleavage is now considered an accessory, but I didn't want to send the wrong message on a first date. Since my date was in advertising, he'd probably appreciate something more fashion forward and colorful than a drab conservative look.

Do you do this? Do you try to match your attire not only to the venue, but to the man? And of course, it has to be congruent with who you are.

Why not wear whatever you darned well feel like, no matter what you know about the man? Why try to wear something that you think he'll find appealing and similar to the style you think he'd find comfortable?

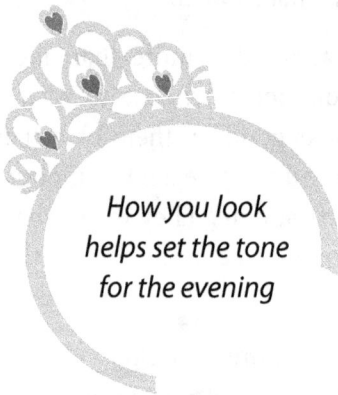

*How you look helps set the tone for the evening*

The answer: to build rapport quickly. To begin the evening, and perhaps the relationship, without friction. We know men are visual. How you look helps set the tone for the evening. Of course, how you both act and what you both say play a huge part.

In college I took a psychology course on Neurolinguistic Programing (NLP). A mouthful, I know. The concepts were initially developed to help therapists build rapport quickly with patients so they would relax and not hold back expressing their thoughts. The work has now been adapted and taught to help people build rapport with others, whether in personal relationships or for business.

One of the key tenets of NLP is to initially match the behaviors and language of the person with whom you are speaking. While I find this can easily be overdone and seem almost mocking and manipulative, done subtly it does get people to open up and relax. So my theory of wearing clothing that my date would find to his taste fits into this matching practice. While I clearly want to be myself, I also know the importance — especially on a first date — of building rapport.

How do you strategically choose to build rapport? Do you plan your outfit based on wanting to look and feel good, as well as taking what you know about your date into consideration? What factors do you consider as you plan your "look" — especially for a first date?

# How do you know he's interested in you?

According to my blog reports, this is a phrase many people search when finding my blog.

I only wish I had the answer.

It is much easier to identify how he shows he's not interested, as I detailed in "12 signs that he won't be asking for a second date" (page 25).

But knowing he is interested? That's a whole different story, and one I don't feel particularly adept at deciphering.

For example, a guy and I had a few email exchanges and a nice phone conversation. He seemed engaged during our first-date dinner, asking me questions, keeping eye contact and sharing his stories and feelings. We occasionally touched the other's hands when we talked. We strolled around the shopping area after dinner, but we didn't hold hands.

At my car he hugged me goodbye and planted a kiss

on my lips. There was no talk of a second date, we just said we enjoyed ourselves and went our separate ways. I was ambiguous about seeing him again but decided to try some recently read advice and try a second date, if he wanted. I wrote him a nice thank you email and suggested we might do another outing.

He wrote back a nice email telling me he enjoyed meeting me but there was no spark for him and asked if we could be pals.

So while there were no flashing green lights that he was interested in me, there were no red lights saying he wanted out of there during dinner. And why would you kiss someone on the lips if you had no interest in them? Was it a test to see if I'd play tonsil hockey with him? It was just a quick smack.

Before I've experienced conflicting signals like this, I'd say "Duh. He emails you regularly. He calls you every few days. He says nice things about you. He asks you to do things with him. He talks about doing future things with you. He touches you respectfully. Maybe he kisses you and/or brings you flowers or small gifts."

But we know that someone could do all of these things and not want a relationship with you, just a booty call. So how is a gal to know how to interpret these things?

I wish I knew.

# "I'm a nerd!"

So said the professor with a Ph.D. and several masters degrees. My Google search revealed a page (not written by him) that called him "a famed professor" in his area of study. Other sites also lauded him. So I thought perhaps he was being modest when saying he was a nerd as he pursued me by sweet, thoughtful emails and phone calls.

His initial email said he was from out of state — 2000 miles away — but was planning to relocate to my area. I am a sucker for a man with good writing skills, so I responded and soon a vigorous email and phone conversation was launched.

When I met him a week after his first email, I saw that he was telling the truth. Can you imagine a 56-year-old Steve Urkel? I'm afraid the similarities were scary. Instead of hiked-up pants, he wore an ill-fitting patterned jacket with clashing shirt. His hunched shoulders suggested a form of osteoporosis or some other back malady. But as I stood straighter, so did he, so it seemed more habit than affliction.

He had braces, which seemed to be helping pull in his buck teeth and closing the gap of several missing ones. This also explained, in part, his lisp. His amblyopia, or lazy eye, kept me guessing which eye to address.

He'd changed his already-scheduled trip to my area for other matters to arrive a day earlier so we could get to know each other. But within a short time I knew there was no romantic future for us, no matter how interesting a writer he was. During lunch I asked him questions in his areas of expertise. I deflected his flirting to other topics or ignored it.

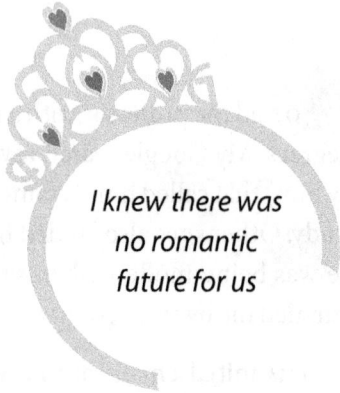

*I knew there was no romantic future for us*

This was more difficult when in an uncrowded area he kissed me. Luckily it was a brief peck, and I pulled away quickly. When he tried to take my hand I did not respond. I found it a challenge to brush off his advances. I didn't want to be rude, as he was a nice man who'd gone considerably out of his way and at added expense to come meet me. But I didn't want to encourage him by seeming to return his ardor.

Ironically, he told me he had to beat off women in his home city. While I recognize he had many inner strengths, was I shallower than his local women who may not have been put off by the outer trappings? Or was he delusional? I've always said treasures can come in imperfect wrappings, but something beyond the physical was not attractive to me. Was it a kind of neediness, bordering on desperation? Was it his continual trying to brush up against me I found off-putting? His flirting despite my giving him no cues that I was interested? Yes, all of the above.

So what to do? Tell the truth, of course, with as much caring and sensitivity as possible. I wrote him what I thought was a kind email, thanking him for his efforts to meet me, and for his generosity taking me to lunch, but saying I didn't feel we were a romantic match, and I'd be honored if he'd allow me to be his friend. I received a terse email back, "I do not think we should waste our time being friends." Obviously, what I felt was a gentle email still smarted. Having been on the receiving end of such emails, I can understand it is never easy to be rejected, no matter how kindly the other tries to put it.

*Make sure to download your free eBook* Attract Your Next Great Mate: Dating Advice From Top Relationship Experts *at www.DatingGoddess.com/ freebie*

# Playgirl glory

It took five months of occasional email exchanges to finally meet. It was worth the wait.

Why so long? He had been traveling the world for a non-profit project he founded. He was in the States infrequently during the past year, and even more rarely at his home in my area.

*It was worth the wait.*

As part of getting to know each other, he sent me a link to his project's Web site where I learned more about him. Armed with his unique full name, it was easy to Google him.

Through this sleuthing I uncovered that he had been not only a Marine fighter pilot — but also a Playgirl "Real Man of the Month!" Granted, that was nearly three decades ago. During our first phone conversation, I commented on his Web page. He said laughingly, "If

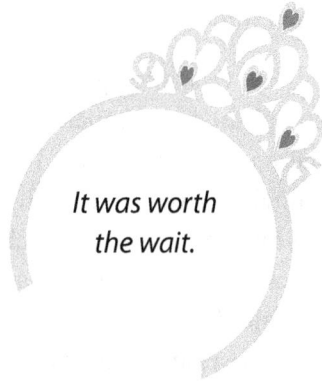

you get me drunk enough I'll tell you some stories that I couldn't put on the page."

"Will that include the Playgirl story?" I asked playfully.

A loud laugh erupted. "How'd you find that?" I told him Google was generous. I added that I'd like to see a copy. He said, "Don't bother buying one of those old issues. The staple hid my glory." Now it was my turn to burst into laughter.

He was intelligent, humble, funny, educated, accomplished, passionate about his project, interested in me, and a good listener. We set a coffee date for the next day. He arrived smartly dressed and greeted me with a big hug and a kiss on the cheek. The 90 minutes passed quickly until he had to leave for another commitment. He said he'd like to see me again. He called 30 minutes after we separated to say how much he enjoyed our time together and was looking forward to the next time.

Will the Playgirl Marine activist work out? One never knows. But at the least it will be a fun adventure getting to know him.

BTW, to the coffee date I brought a staple remover. ☺

# First-encounter mismatch

An Adventures in Delicious Dating After 40 reader wrote:

> *What do you do if it is obvious in the first 5 minutes that there is not a fit? Do you sludge through the evening or cut your losses early? I don't mean to be cruel but sometimes it seems to be worse to lead the person on.*

Good question. This is why I nearly always insist on a coffee meeting for the first encounter. Several times I was very grateful I'd insisted on that, as it can be challenging to be nice to someone who obviously has different priorities around grooming, eye contact, or dental hygiene. As you say, feigning interest just sends mixed messages and will cause more pain when you do pull the plug. However, that's no excuse to be rude.

If the coffee goes well, it can extend to several hours, or at worst will make you both look forward to the next rendezvous.

So if you'd made the mistake of offering or accepting a dinner invitation for the first meeting, I think your best bet would be to beg off with, "I'm sorry, I know we said we'd have dinner together, but my plans changed. I need to leave in a few minutes, but I did want to meet you, and we can have a quick drink." You don't have to say, "My plans changed just now that I've met you and found out that you shaved 20 years off your age," or "... since you posted pictures from your 20s and you're now 50!" or "...it's obvious you haven't seen a dentist in 20 years," or "...I really prefer to date a man who understands the importance of good grooming." Be as gracious as possible, and if s/he probes, try to be nebulous.

Be prepared that he may become huffy, "I got dressed up and drove down here because you said we'd have dinner." Just apologize for the unforseen plan change, but don't promise a do over. How he reacts will tell you a lot about the man, so don't get down and dirty even if the other does. Even though you'll never see him again, remember there is dating karma (at least I believe so). What goes around comes around, so if you are mean to this person, someone will be mean to you in the future. Don't go there.

But do go to the nearest exit as soon as you can graciously do so. Twenty to thirty minutes should do the trick. If he contacts you afterward, just send a nice email saying that you didn't feel a romantic connection. This may sting a bit, but if you do it nicely, it will sting less. And it will sting way less than if you stayed around and pretended to be interested in someone you're not.

# Assuming privileges

When you talk to a potential suitor regularly for more than a few weeks before meeting, a false sense of intimacy can develop. In flirty or soul-baring emails and/ or phone conversations, you can begin to feel a budding emotional connection to the other.

Then when you do meet, there is an odd closeness. You feel you know someone who you've not met — essentially a stranger. There is a tendency to fast-forward to physical affection that would have taken longer (usually) to develop if you'd had less pre-meeting phone time.

You may have developed a fondness for the person through what and how he shared. So when he takes your hand in his, it seems an abnormal mix of comfort and newness. You both are more comfortable touching during this first meeting than you would be on a first date with someone you hadn't talked to a lot before meeting.

Unfortunately, I've found this unnatural familiarity leads to behaviors that assume privileges too soon. Strong relationships are forged over time, not jumped into quickly.

It's like cooking a thick, juicy chicken breast. If you

just flash sear the outside without proper cooking time, the inside is raw. Not only is that unappealing, it's unhealthy. However, if the chicken is poached, roasted or grilled longer the result is a succulent, tender, delicious dish.

I guess I'm hungry! But the metaphor is apt.

I've been taken aback by men who I've talked to for a few weeks before meeting who've assumed we'd sleep together on our first date. Some of my pals say that this is an assumption many dating men have, even if you've only talked once! But even men who talk about the importance of respecting a woman, and wanting to get to know me, can act this way. It certainly doesn't feel respectful when a man assumes intimacy that is many steps beyond your current comfort level — and you have to repeatedly tell him to slow down.

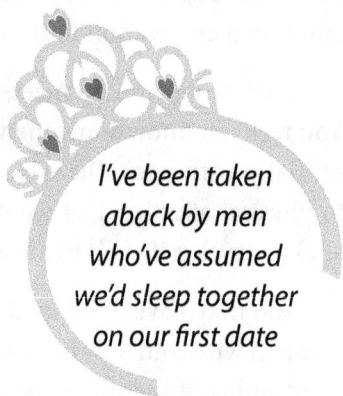

*I've been taken aback by men who've assumed we'd sleep together on our first date*

When sharing this observation with a sage gal pal she said that all some men need to feel the gauge is reading "full speed ahead" is a woman who shows some interest. If a man is not adept at reading a woman's signs — which can be either blatant or subtle — he moves forward at the pace he wants, misinterpreting — or ignoring — the woman's words and body language. This can be true for men who may be astute at reading people in other settings, so I'm not sure if it's obtuseness or self-focusedness.

No matter what the cause, it is disappointing to learn that someone you became fond of over the phone can be an oaf in person. Which is why I try to meet a new man within a week or so of a first email or phone call. There is less time to build up false intimacy and overblown expectations.

# Clothes make the man

Nearly eighteen months ago a man sent me an email on a dating site where I wasn't a member. Although he was in the right geographic, age and height range, his pictures showed an unsmiling, sunglass-wearing, goatee-sporting man in a sports-team T-shirt holding up a newspaper with an unreadable headline. Huh? This is the best picture the man thought represented him to his future match?

Since I wasn't a member of the site, I couldn't read his email but was allowed to send a site-generated "No thank you" response.

A year later he showed up on another site where I could see he'd looked at my profile several times. After several months of seeing his picture appear in my "who's seen you list" I became curious. He'd posted a few more pictures on this site and he looked less thug-like than he did in the one pic on the previous site.

I finally joined the original site for a month to read messages from a few men who looked interesting. I read his old message and found it was articulate, romantic, sweet, charming. His writing style was far above nearly all others. It was specific to me and items in my profile, not pro-forma.

He'd included his Yahoo address, so I wrote a brief email saying "hi" — even after all these months. He enthusiastically replied, saying he had given up hope of ever meeting me and was excited I had reached out. We began a week-long phone and IM flirt that culminated in lunch.

He appeared at the restaurant in a cashmere polo shirt, nice jeans and good shoes. He was tall, neat, clean — and handsome! He had a muscled build, clearly chiseled from regular gym visits. He appeared younger than his 56 years. He looked like the men I covet — why didn't he show this side in his pictures? I would have leapt on his email!

I was awaiting him in a reception chair outside the restaurant and waived as he approached. I rose to greet him, to which he said "Wait, wait, don't move. I want to savor this moment." Very sweet. After we hugged hello, he presented me with a gift bag of tulips, a stuffed bear, and a greeting card stating "Thinking of you," along with a handwritten message. Wow!

He was charming, funny, intelligent, engaging and gentlemanly during lunch and afterward when we sat in his car listening to music while we continued our discussion. Even after being together 3 hours, we didn't want to part, but I knew it best to not let a first encounter go on too long. He asked if he could see me again. Is the Pope Catholic? Of course! He was so much of

*My heart was beginning to melt*

what I'd been looking for, my heart was beginning to melt. We set a dinner date for the next night.

This was a good lesson for me. I have written before about how important good profile pictures are, as well as how photos are just a rough facsimile of the real thing. (See the *Winning at the Online Dating Game: Stack the Deck in Your Favor* book.) I have frequently dismissed approaches from men who have unappealing photos thinking if they aren't smart enough to know the value of a photo on a first impression then they aren't for me. However this man was so much better in person than his photo. His smile was so engaging, why wouldn't he post a smiling pic? Or in nice clothes, rather than his around-the-house look? Who knows?

But I know I'm glad I gave this one a second chance. In fact, I now kick myself for missing out knowing him for 18 months. I console myself by knowing I've learned a lot about myself and men in the last 18 months and may not have been ready to receive him in my life at that time. If he continues to be the gem he appears to be, I am ready to receive him with open arms — for more of those yummy hugs he gave at lunch.

# *Yummy is as yummy does*

When my friends ask if whatever man I'm seeing is handsome, I commonly respond, "If I saw him from across the room, I wouldn't say, 'Who's that yummy guy?' But the more I'm with him, the yummier he gets."

Men seem to become cuter as their personalities emerge. A man who isn't George Clooney handsome can be irresistible because of his humor, insights, introspection, boldness, thoughtfulness, intelligence, smile, presence and self-confidence. In fact, some of the sexiest and most attractive men I've known wouldn't be considered handsome if you just saw their pictures. But within minutes of being with them, they've won you to their side.

*Within minutes they've won you to their side*

And somehow men who are attracted to you and treat you like a queen grow more appealing. Some guys know this, especially if they aren't particularly good looking. If women don't naturally flirt with him, a smart man makes himself alluring by consciously treating a woman so she feels special, appreciated and sexy — as long as he's not slimy about it.

So even if a man isn't initially tantalizing, give him a chance to improve his yummy-quotient. You may just find a wonderful gentleman hiding under an ordinary exterior — and you'll end up besotted nonetheless.

# Extricating yourself from a dud date

There are good dates, ambivalent dates, bad dates, and sometimes dates that are none of the above, just clearly not encounters with someone who is in any way a match. They can be painful when you, for manners' sake, must stay longer than you would prefer.

After a few email and phone conversations with a smart, articulate man who made me laugh, I accepted his lunch invitation, even though I generally start with only coffee. I rued not sticking with this rule!

When we met he at the bookstore in an urban downtown, a broad smile crossed his face, which generally means a man likes my looks. He asked where I wanted to go, then overruled my suggestion for a nearby restaurant and choose a Chinese one he wanted to try instead. Since he said he was treating, I thought I shouldn't quibble.

He ordered soup and we agreed to split the entrée. Then he launched into not only his life story, but his father's story as well, then picked up his own at his birth! Since he was talking non-stop, he barely touched his soup. When the entrée arrived, I dug in. I'd finished my meal and he was still working on his soup — and we were only up to age 11 — and he is now 61!

Since I was then ready to go and he hadn't begun his entrée, I saw I was going to have to listen to a recounting of 50 years while sitting idly. I knew by now I had no interest in this man, not only because he was prattling on in minute detail about his life, but he made nearly

> *I was going to have to listen to a recounting of 50 years.*

no eye contact during his monologue. So it didn't matter that over his shoulder I was watching the street scene out the window to entertain myself, as he never saw my gaze. Since he had to turn his head to look at me, I made sure I was looking at him on the few occasions he made eye contact.

Finally I said something about his meal being cold and I think it clicked that he had been doing 100% of the talking for the last hour. So he said, "Well, that's my life story. What has brought you to where you are today?" A pretty lame question. I answered it as best I could, and within 3 minutes he'd changed the subject.

Since the server had long ago brought the check,

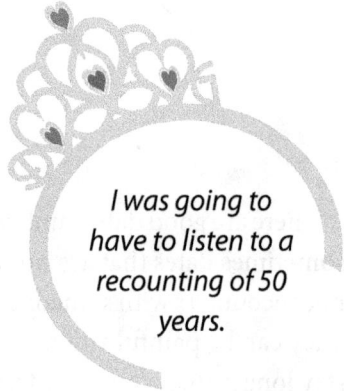

I thought the best way to signal I was done was to say, "I'm going to visit the ladies room, then when you're done we can depart." When I returned, he'd paid the check and yet he lingered longer at the table. When it looked like he'd stopped eating, I gathered my things, then after a few more minutes stood up. We walked toward the parking lot, passing some businesses on the way. I had told him I had an errand to run at one of these shops, so he accompanied me. I was surprised he elongated the date, as I had no indication he had the slightest interest in me. I searched for my item and he ambled about the shop.

After paying, we walked toward the parking lot together. His car was parked closer than mine, so he peeled off toward his, with nary a word. So when I saw he had no intention of walking me to mine, I said, "Thank you for lunch. It was good to meet you." He said, "Yes it was good to meet you, too." By neither of us saying anything about seeing each other again, it was understood that neither of us was interested.

Could/should I have extricated myself when I was done with my meal and knew I had no interest in him? Some would say yes, justifying this rudeness by saying straightforward directness is best. Besides, I was never going to see him again, so what did it matter? It would save wasting an hour with someone who was clueless.

But I believe in dating karma. If I want someone to treat me kindly, even if he has no interest in me, then I must do the same. Leaving while someone is still dining is rude — really rude.

Now perhaps he thought I was a dud and was trying to entertain me with his long-winded story. We'll never know.

# Control freak or detail oriented?

In the 18 months between when my ex left and I started dating, I had plenty of time to consider what I wanted in my next man. One of my realizations was I planned 99% of our outings in my marriage. I wanted a man who would take the time to plan, as I was burnt out from it, and I saw it as a way to show he cared.

I quickly found a planner in one of the first men I met online. After our initial contact I told him the next day I was departing for a six-day business trip. I'd only be available by email because of my tight schedule. We flirted by email several times a day for four days. On day five, he asked me to join him for dinner when I returned. We agreed on when and where.

He was the first stranger with whom I'd had a date. (The previous "dates" were with colleagues.) He did things that no man has done since. My friends were either impressed or incredulous. This guy was a uber-planner!

While still on my trip, he emailed me a PDF of the restaurant's menu, saying if I had an idea what I might want (e.g., fish, beef, lamb, chicken), he would pre-order the wine so it would be ready for us.

On the appointed evening, I was nervous since this was the first time I'd had a date with someone I didn't already know. I obsessed about what to wear. I must have changed clothes six times.

*I must have changed clothes six times.*

He greeted me at the restaurant bar with a hug and a gift of two CDs. He said that we could listen to them while cooking together sometime. Cool.

After a drink, the maître d' told us our table was ready. We were escorted to a secluded candle-lit, semi-circular banquette. The manager came over and greeted my date by name. I thought he must come here often.

Later I learned that my guy had come to the restaurant earlier and discussed this evening with the manager. He told him he was bringing a special lady and wanted the evening to be memorable. He'd asked for the best server working that night. Then he chose the most romantic table in that server's section. The manager assured him the table would be reserved for him and that he'd inform his server to go out of his way to make it a special event.

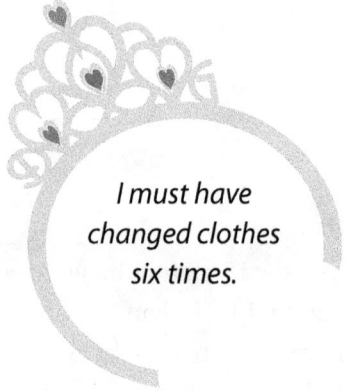

We lingered over dinner for five hours, laughing and talking. We were the first couple in the restaurant and the last to leave. He walked me to my car and we ended with a hug.

Did I want to see him again? I wasn't drawn to him physically, but he made me laugh, and I liked being treated well. I decided I'd see him again. Why? Because he went to so much thought and effort to make the evening distinctive and me feel pampered.

What did I learn? That I like a man who pays attention to details, who goes to some effort to make me feel special and that a little thought can overcome a lack of initial physical attraction. He scratched an itch I had and evidently I scratched one for him.

Some friends thought he was controlling and anal retentive to put so much effort into this first encounter. I thought it was sweet and made me feel special. So what works for one may not for another.

We went out for six weeks, and he treated me well, but only one other time did he put the same thought into a date as he had that first one. When I realized we weren't a long-term match for many reasons, I told him I didn't think we should continue going out. He still wanted to see me, but I knew he wouldn't see other women if I agreed. We continue to stay in touch, and we occasionally see a play, movie or have dinner together, but as pals.

The lesson to share is that behavior trumps physicality. However, if after giving it a chance if you still aren't a match, don't hang on as it's not fair to either one of you. Release each other to find your true match.

# Are you a generous conversationalist?

I had the opportunity to be with a handful of extremely smart, highly accomplished executive women friends. I noticed two things about our conversations:

1. Some of the women add to the conversation only what they think would be of interest to others, not whatever crosses their mind at the moment.

2. Some of the women are very generous listeners, not judging what comes out of another's mouth.

While I count myself in the first category, I became painfully aware I am not always in the second. It made me think of my conversation habits on a date and how I resonate with dates who have a similar conversation style.

When on a date, do you share what you think might be interesting to the guy? Even if you are sharing a story about yourself and your life, it can still be of interest to him if he is interested in you. However, when the conversation becomes a monologue and the other shows waning interest, you need to switch the focus to him or a mutually interesting topic.

I work to be conscious of what falls out of my mouth so I'm not prattling on. I also work to bring up topics that I think might be of interest to others, to not delve into fine details unless someone asks, and to not monopolize the conversation. However, I can also spew out comments meant to be witty or funny that are ill conceived and therefore not well received.

*I've developed a low tolerance for those who aren't pithy*

Perhaps because of my focus on being pithy, I've developed a low tolerance for those who aren't. Which brings us to my struggles with category 2. On dates I try to be on my best behavior and if my date is belaboring a point, I work to give him some grace. But if he repeatedly recounts great details about things like the golf game he watched on TV or his sister-in-law's brother's gallbladder problems, I'm out of there.

I believe you have conversation responsibilities in relationships, even budding ones. Optimally, you are both a conscious talker, focusing on what might engage the other and sharing air time somewhat equally, as well as a generous listener.

One of these astute women friends pointed out that even if someone you care for is talking about something in which you have no interest, you listen fully — because it is of interest to them. Her comment struck me as incredibly mature, evolved and loving. I saw I have some work to do to increase my generous, loving listening skills.

How about you? Are you a considerate and conscious talker? And a generous listener?

# *Yuck!*

feel soiled, sullied, icky. Bad. Horrible. I unknowingly betrayed a good, long-time friend. "How?" you ask. Here's the story.

A few months ago a man emailed me from a dating site new to me. We struck up a nice IM conversation. He hadn't posted a pic, so I asked for one and he promptly obliged. He was average looking, having features similar to many midlife men in my area. But I was drawn by his wit, intelligence and sweetness.

After a few days of IM and phone conversations, we agreed to lunch. Immediately upon meeting, he kissed me briefly on the lips. A tad forward, I thought. While we stood in line for a table he took my hand. We had a nice lunch conversation. He was better looking in person than his picture. During the after-lunch stroll he put his arm around my waist. After a half block, he stopped and kissed me. Again, I thought a tad early for my taste. We walked some more, and he left me at my car with a promise to call.

He IMed within minutes of my returning home. He called on his way home from work. We talked about getting together again in a few days. He continued to IM frequently. Two days after the lunch date, we had plans to go to the movies, but he called to say he had an emergency with his teenage daughter so would have to reschedule. We IMed, then talked the next day. Then I got the email quoted in "Is it affection or obsession?" (in the *Dipping Your Toe in the Dating Pool: Dive In Without Belly Flopping* book).

Today my long-time friend was over and we were chatting. About 18 months ago she married a man she'd met online a year before, on a different site than the one on which this guy found me. I'd met her husband briefly at their wedding. He was a normal-looking guy without any unusual physical characteristics. I focused on her because she was so resplendent in her wedding regalia.

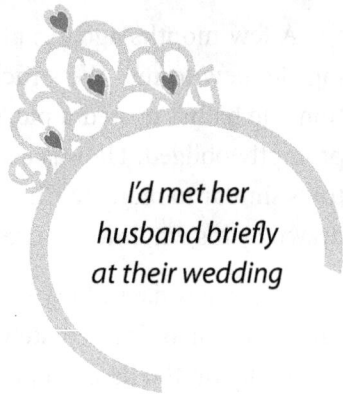

> *I'd met her husband briefly at their wedding*

In our conversation today I realized I didn't know what her husband did for a living and where he worked. She told me. I said, "That's interesting. I went out once a few months ago with a man who does that in the same part of town. And they share the same common first name." We continued the comparison. I told her of his quick affectionate behavior. She said, "My husband did that on our first date." Hmmm. She asked if I had his pic. Thanks to my trusty Date-A-Base (in the *Multidating Responsibly: Play the Field Without Being A Player* book) I did! Plus a copy of his profile and some emails.

The picture staring back at her was, as you've guessed, her husband. I felt sadness and anger for my friend. How could he do this to her? She deserved a great guy, not a two-timing philanderer. She was upset, but not as much as I would have been. It seems he did this when they were dating, in what they'd both promised was an exclusive relationship. She thought he had grown up. Obviously he hadn't.

In the past he'd explained his addiction to the pursuit of women. He claimed he took it no farther than kissing, and usually cut it off within a few weeks. His self-esteem needed to be constantly reassured he was able to attract women. He knew he had a problem. He thought he could fix this himself, so he kept making excuses for not seeking counseling. Obviously, he was wrong.

My friend was actually grateful that it was me he'd attempted to woo, as she now had proof of his indiscretions, rather than her suspicions and his vehement denials. He couldn't lie his way out of this any longer. If he didn't agree to counseling immediately, she was leaving him.

I have a mix of remorse, sadness, anger, and in a strange way, gratefulness that I could help catch this Lothario. She should be with a fabulous guy who adores her and would never consider cheating. If this Casanova won't grow up, I hope she jettisons him so she can have a great man.

To show what a mature individual she is in the face of this information, she holds no malice toward me, acknowledging that I met him so briefly previously I couldn't be expected to remember him out of context of being by her side, let alone on a dating site. She was actually appreciative that he hadn't recognized me either, so she could have the evidence she needed to confront him.

I know there are myriad stories of married people listing themselves on dating sites. I have encountered only one other who I discovered was married — thanks to a mutual friend — and I declined to meet him. Had I known this one was, I would not have met him either. I don't like unwittingly being the other woman.

Looking back, there were no signs that pointed to him being in a relationship. He wasn't wearing a wedding ring. Since my friend retained her maiden name and I didn't remember her husband's last name from the one time I saw it on the wedding invitation, even his using his real last name didn't raise a red flag.

I guess this shows that it is good to meet a man's friends before getting too serious and hope one of them pulls you aside if something is amiss. I have no idea how I would have found out, as he could have easily kept up his ruse for months since she travels a lot. And I don't know how she would have had indisputable proof if we hadn't been chit-chatting about her hubby.

# *Glass half full or empty?*

On a first date, a man asked if I was a glass-half-full or half-empty kind of gal. Although a tad trite, no one else had asked directly if I was optimistic or pessimistic. I wondered who would admit to the latter, although I know some are attracted to others who share a negative world view.

*No one else had asked directly if I was optimistic or pessimistic.*

I am drawn to positive people — those who aren't stopped by obstacles, but look for ways around them. People who don't focus on what's missing as long as what is present brings you satisfaction.

My friend, the outstanding motivational speaker W Mitchell was in a blazing motorcycle accident, leaving him with devastating burns over 65% of his body. Four years later he survived a paralyzing plane crash.

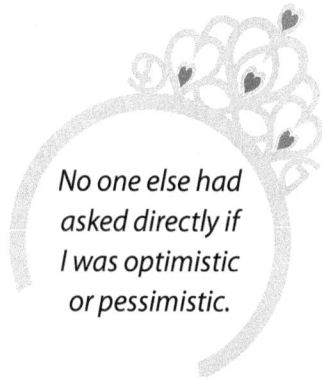

He learned to choose to look at the positives in life rather than the negatives. In his speeches, he says, "Before the accidents, I could do 10,000 things. Now I can do 9000. I can bemoan the 1000 I can't do now, or I can relish the 9000." Mitchell definitely sees the glass half full.

I dated a man for months who focused on the few things we didn't enjoy together, rather than the dozens of things we did. I can understand if your love doesn't like to do things that are important to you — things that are critical to your enjoying life. But if your sweetie likes to do lots of what you like to do, then why focus on the few things you don't share a love for? This man was a half-empty kind of guy.

Which are you — half-empty or half-full? Why? And if you're like me — mostly half-full although there are some things that I absolutely must have in my life — what won't you compromise, no matter how many things you have in common?

# Ambiva-date

He was funny and intelligent during the 4 calls prior to our drink date. His pictures in his online profile were a bit fuzzy, but nothing odious. Our conversation assured me he wasn't a sex maniac, egomaniac, nor a maniac of any kind. Although it did give me some pause that he was 57 and never married.

We decided to meet in the bar of a nice nearby hotel. I felt I'd sufficiently vetted him to ensure we'd have an enjoyable time.

I didn't recognize him at first, but he was the only lone man approximating his picture who seemed to be looking for someone. I said his name and he nodded yes.

I suggested he pick a place in the sparsely populated bar. He choose two comfortable chairs both facing out, with a small table in between. So we would be sitting facing the same direction, not each other. Odd choice, I thought, for wanting to get to know each other. I moved my chair to face him. He left his facing out.

He picked up the voluminous drink menu and began scouring it. The waitress came over and we told her we had no idea. He spent a while examining the choices. The waitress came again. He ordered his drink, then passed the menu to me. Perhaps I'm old fashioned, but has "ladies first" gone out of style?

> *The conversation wasn't strained, but neither was it effortless.*

We chatted for a while, picking up some themes from our previous conversations. No flirting. It felt like I was passing time with a seat mate on an airplane or someone waiting in a hotel lobby. No seeming interest in exploring what we might have in common. The conversation wasn't strained, but neither was it effortless. Some laughter punctuated our discussion of the news, investments, experiences being childless, and other inconsequential things. I tried to think of questions that would lead to more meaningful discussion, but my mind was blank.

After 90 minutes, he made an excuse to go. Fine with me. He opened the bill folder to display our check. I said, "What's our damage?" as I always offer to pay my share. Ninety-eight percent of the men have said, "I've got it." He did not. I put in my money. I arose to don my coat. No help from him. He didn't offer to walk me to my car in the underground parking lot. We muttered something like, "Nice to meet you," hugged briefly as we parted ways.

When people ask me about my dating life, they assume it is all fine dining, dancing, and scintillating conversation. More than half the men I have gone out with have been "one-date onlys." The above describes why. There is no spark, no interest in really getting to spend more time together. And perhaps I'm overly scrutinising, but things like manners count a lot to me on a first encounter.

Does that mean you shouldn't go out with someone with whom you've had a good connection on the phone? You should go out with anyone you find interesting. But you need to know that this is a common experience. Having a great time with someone is not the norm. Ambivalence is the norm. Appreciate it when you have a great time but don't be upset when you don't. It's all part of the process. Plus, you get a new acquaintance.

# *He suggests getting naked — for the second date!*

It's not what you think. Yes, he suggested getting naked, although he didn't say it that bluntly.

We had a first date three weeks ago. We had talked on the phone once a week for a month, but then we both had foreign travel and we couldn't meet before then. We met for lunch and didn't run out of interesting things to discuss.

Afterward, he left for another 2-week trip, arriving home yesterday and called today. At the end of the hour-long chat he suggested we get together in two weeks when he returns from his next trip. His proposal? We soak in a special enzyme tub for two at his favorite spa, then dinner afterwards.

Hmm. Getting naked on the second date? I don't know.

I know that one can wear a bathing suit even in a

private spa tub, but it seems a bit prudish. But then getting naked with a man — even knowing sex is not expected nor implied — seems rushing things a bit. There would be no hanky panky, as an attendant would be regularly bringing us a special tea and cold compresses for our foreheads.

If this were Europe, it would be no big deal for most people. But many Americans, including me, are a tad modest at first.

Is this a test to see where I am on the naturalist/prude continuum? An opportunity for him to check out the "goods" before becoming too involved? I don't know. In the hours we've spent on the phone he's never been inappropriate, suggestive, or even flirty. In fact, during lunch I wasn't sure if he'd contact me again because there was no flirtation on his part. So he's not being a letch — I don't think — by suggesting a couple's soak.

This has taken me by surprise, as I've not had anyone else suggest an activity so, well, intimate, so early in the dating cycle. Before I agree to any part of his invitation, I will tell him I'm a bit uncomfortable with this activity so early in our getting to know each other. I'll suggest that we either have separate soaks, or just skip the spa this time and do something else together that entails keeping our clothes on.

Have you received an invitation for something a bit too intimate for your comfort level in the early stages of getting to know a man? If so, how did you deal with it?

# *Falling for your date*

T he other day I fell. Not *for* my date, but *on* my date. And a first date at that.

It was pretty embarrassing, as well as painful. I was all cuted up, in a form-fitting top, sassy skirt, patterned hose, 2-inch heels — not too high. I had nothing — absolutely no alcohol — to drink. We were dining at a table raised above the floor by two small steps. There was low lighting.

When I excused myself to go to the ladies room I didn't see one of the steps and went down hard. My cute self was splayed on the floor. Luckily, my skirt wasn't wrapped around my head.

The waiters and manager ran over to see if I was hurt. Mostly, it was my ego that was bruised, as well as some abrasions on my shins and thigh. My hose had a little tear. Otherwise, I was fine.

Interestingly, my date — seated a few feet away — didn't get up to come to my aid. He turned around in his chair to face me and asked if I was okay as I scrambled to rise and regain what was left of my dignity.

In my four years of dating, I've not had another

similarly embarrassing mishap. It made me think of how it telegraphs a lot by how we react when calamity happens to us or our date.

I was shaken and embarrassed, but tried to shrug it off. I continued to the ladies room with my head held high. Only when in the well-lit restroom did I see my shins had some open wounds which were oozing a little blood. When I went back to the table, I joked about my klutziness.

It told me a lot about my date that he didn't rise to help me up, dust me off, or see if I was OK. He just asked from his chair. Did he think he was preventing further embarrassment by not making a fuss? Did he see that I was already vertical so there wasn't much he could do? Since I said I was fine there was no need to come closer to see?

I don't know about you, but if I saw someone nearby go down, whether I knew them or not, I'd like to think I'd go to their aid. And if I knew them, I know I would. So for my date to not bother to come check on me was a flag that said we had different perspectives of what was important in dealing with people. And specifically, about people in some distress.

Now I don't recommend you fall down as a way to test your date's values around helping you if you were in trouble. But if you do have an unfortunate mishap, notice what he does or doesn't do and how you feel about it.

And try to keep your skirt down as you fall.

# First date — with two chaperones!

When he said he wanted to fly in to meet me, we didn't intend for it to be a chaperoned event. But it ended up being one — with two escorts!

Thanks to a friend's largesse, my date and I were invited to accompany him and another friend to a professional basketball team, for which he had comp tickets. So my two friends ended up being the equivalent of my brothers, checking out my date by trying to engage him in conversation. Un-

*My date was more interesting on the phone than in person.*

fortunately, my date was more interesting on the phone than in person so his flippant and one-word responses to my friends' conversation starters stopped any attempt to bring him into the discussion.

While I don't recommend it for a first date, your friends' interactions with your date tell you volumes that you don't see when it's just the two of you. Yes, alone I noticed his lack of eye contact or any apparent interest in knowing anything about me. But it was even more glaring watching him with my friends. They graciously tried to include him and draw him into discussions (I love them for doing this!), yet he seemed bent on staying an outsider. Was he threatened by their clear camaraderie with me and each other? Our easy laughing and joking with each other? This is common friend behavior and if he couldn't allow himself to be engaged, then he's not the guy for me.

What have you learned about someone you've begun to date by their interactions (or lack thereof!) with your friends?

# *Being the practice date*

I almost canceled. Why? Was he odious and self-absorbed on the phone? Sex obsessed? Foul mouthed?

No. If he were, I wouldn't have agreed to coffee.

His emails showed he was smart; his call was interesting, incorporating current events. He could converse about different topics without being obnoxiously opinionated or emphatic.

So why wasn't I excited about meeting him? I didn't find anything I was curious to know more about him. He'd been retired for 8 years, although he was still in his 50's.

I met him anyway, although I was thinking of ways to put him off up until an hour before we met. The bottom line was I just didn't feel we had enough in common to see him again. I know it is terrible to make this kind of judgment before even meeting him. I encourage others to meet a guy for coffee if there are no glaring red flags in the pre-meeting vetting. Yet here I was violating my own advice.

The conversation meandered through many topics. He stayed focused, didn't complain about his ex, didn't

ramble about his kids, or friends of friends, or his resume. He tracked with the conversation and made relevant comments.

I vacillated between thinking, "I would have coffee with him again," to "How do I tell him I don't feel
a spark?" It turned out to be a moot battle in my head,
as he didn't ask to see me again. I learned I was the first
woman he'd gone out with after his divorce last year.
He'd only been on the dating site a month, and I was "an
experiment."

I was his practice date!

I've learned I was the practice date — the first post-
divorce encounter — for two other men. One was so
needy he determined I was "The One" within 10 minutes. The other was more grounded and he became one
of my treasures.

I'd done it many times myself when I was first dating. I'd accept coffee invitations from nearly any man
whose profile and conversation were interesting. Those
practice dates helped build my confidence and comfort
around men who were deciding if they were interested
in me or not.

Have you known you were a man's practice date
soon after his divorce/widowhood? If so, did you treat
him differently than other men who seemed more experienced?

# Opening the kimono

We'd been talking for a few weeks before meeting. I'm not fond of trying to kindle a relationship with someone living 1000 miles away, but he had certain rare attributes I've been looking for in a partner, but unable to find locally.

He arranged to stop in my city on his way home from a business trip. At dinner, he was as charming in person as on the phone and IM. We laughed and talked easily as we already knew a good deal about each other. He was a perfect gentleman, sharing his delight about our meeting and never trying to force more intimacy than a first meeting warranted.

I picked him up the next day and we visited some mutually interesting sites, had a leisurely walk, lunch, and got to know each other better. We both realized the face-to-face meeting shifts the interactions.

Mid-afternoon, he said, "I want to disclose certain things I think you should know." He didn't share anything shocking — no not-quite-complete divorce, no baby mamas, no incarceration, no major health issues, no deep indebtedness, no sex-change operation. His disclosures were reasonably normal — a small debt from co-signing a loan for a relative who defaulted, some frustration about growing his business, and a few personal foilables.

I was touched by his forthrightness. I interpreted his initiating sharing his situation as showing he cared and was intending our relationship to be long term. He wanted to put his cards on the table and let me see what I'd be getting into if we went forward.

Perhaps my appreciation for this man's disclosures were a reaction to my last beau's secrecy. Getting information about basic things like how he'd spent his day was always a struggle. This man shared freely.

I realize the sharing may be just the tip of the iceberg and there may be much, much more that has yet to be disclosed. I also realize it could all be made up, but there hasn't been anything that didn't gel. I know, too, that some men use such disclosures as a way to manipulate the woman into trusting them.

I felt none of that with this man. He didn't press me to escalate our connection after he'd shared his information. It did make me feel a bit more fond of him, however.

Have you had someone disclose personal information quickly? If so, did you think it was suspicious or did you appreciate it?

# *Are you easily offended when dating?*

A friend invited me to lunch with her and her 62-year-old sister. "Sis" is dating, although she admitted to only having one date a year, so I use the term "dating" loosely.

Sis shared about her one 2009 date. She'd met the guy online, talked a few times by email and phone, and felt they had enough in common to meet for lunch. Their conversation began pleasantly, until about 20 minutes passed when he said, "I hope you don't mind, but I don't sleep with women on the first date."

She was incensed, threw $20 on the table to cover her lunch and stalked out without saying a word. When he called a few days later to ask what he'd said that was offensive, she responded, "It's clear there's no reason to waste time explaining. Don't call again," and hung up.

My friend asked what I would have done. I said, "Assuming he hadn't been uncouth up to that point, I would have said, 'I'm so glad we're on the same page!' and laughed it off."

I asked Sis why she was offended. "He made an assumption that I was trolling for sex. Assumptions like that are unforgivable."

"I wouldn't have had that interpretation," I responded. "Was there other conversation that suggested sex?"

"No, not prior to that."

*"Was there other conversation that suggested sex?"*

Based on what she'd shared, I felt her response was over the top. In fact, I felt she made assumptions that weren't warranted. We didn't further explore the scenario, but I'm thinking she had some previous experience with a man (or men) who expected sex on the first meeting, or accused her of wanting the same.

The lessons for us all are:

If you get upset over a dating encounter, later check with a friend to see if s/he thinks you overreacted. If so, identify the trigger and where in the past you felt similarly. Most likely your reaction has little to do with the recent experience, and more about something you thought was unjust in the past. You will continue to react inappropriately and repel potential mates until you heal the past, through inner work, either alone or with a counselor.

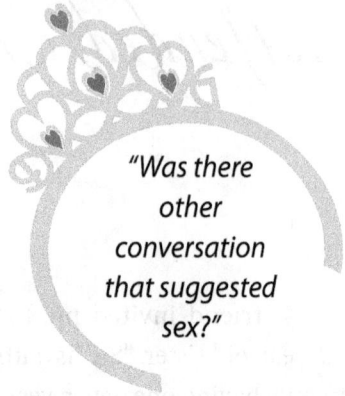

If you are on the receiving end of an overreaction, check with an opposite sex friend to see if you might have unknowingly pushed a button commonly shared by that gender. Or see if your pal thinks what you did warranted the response you received. If your pal thinks your behavior was fine, then write it off to your date being triggered and it had nothing really to do with you. Know that this person has some issues they need to work on and probably best that you not be in the picture while they do.

Have you had someone on a date get incensed with something you thought was innocent?

# *The keys to allure*

ince humankind began, people have been trying to improve their allure. Yet it seems elusive for many, even though some elements seem obvious:

❤ *Attractive appearance.* A willingness to consciously make yourself appealing to those you want to attract. I have no idea, then, why so many online profiles feature hideous pictures. And even with a reasonable picture, why men show up unkempt apparently not passing a mirror before leaving their house or office.

❤ *Pleasant personality.* Charm can trump physical attractiveness. Being complimentary and nice pulls someone to you much more than insults and meanness. Yet millions of people haven't seemed to learn this basic concept.

Yesterday a midlife gal pal and I were comparing dating stories. We shared what we've gleaned that men seem to be drawn to. We examined our own dating success and felt it boiled down to a few key areas.

The men were lonely and happy to have any pleasant, reasonably attractive woman's company. We both qualified with these basic qualities.

But beyond this, we felt there were other behaviors comprising appeal that apparently few women have figured out.

Actively listening. This may seem like a "duh," but the truth is, not many people are truly good listeners, gently asking relevant questions that show interest. Few people have a natural curiosity when it comes to others. Some who do, ask questions that are intrusive or combative, rather than in a gently caring way. Most people respond positively to another who takes a genuine interest in them. By actively listening you can learn a lot about someone. After a few email interactions and a few hours in person, a man told me that I knew more about him than most of his friends. I think I listened better and seemed more interested in him than his friends.

> *This may seem like a "duh."*

In a recent exploratory conversation, a 55-year-old man told me that he'd returned to school to sharpen his skills since he was laid off two years ago. He'd created a summer-focused business and I asked how he supported himself through the winter. He said, "With student loans." That was enough to tell me we were at different places in our lives and I wasn't interested in progressing.

Eye contact. Again, this should be common sense. But I now know that many midlife people feel invisible, marginalized by the lack of people noticing them other than those obligated to do so. If you focus on someone during a conversation that is such an unusual and exhilarating experience for some they are immediately drawn to you.

During the break in my presentation recently, a man came up and asked me a question. He was sort of geeky looking, overweight, and bespectacled. I doubted many woman gave him much attention. I held eye contact during our brief conversation. After my speech, he came up and asked if he could help me pack up and continued to talk with me. I think the eye contact made him feel that someone had noticed him and this was a warm, wonderful, and unusual experience.

So allure can be simple. One does not have to have stunningly good looks to be alluring. Simple sincere behaviors can make you more attractive.

What else would you add to this short list of alluring elements?

# Thank you for using good manners

When leaving my exercise class at an elementary school auditorium, this sign caught my eye. It made me think it ought to be posted at coffee shops to remind daters to use their manners!

Why did this cross my mind?

I had another date that left me scratching my head. I checked with a couple of male pals to see if I had too-high expectations.

"What happened?" you ask.

We'd talked, texted and emailed for a few weeks as we worked out a mutually available evening. There seemed to be a shared interest.

When I arrived at the nearly empty coffee shop, he was sitting at a table typing on his phone. I stood opposite him and said "Hello." He looked up from his phone and said "Hello."

He didn't rise to greet me. I can't remember a date

not rising when I appeared, and then either offer a hand or a hug. Heck, I rise on first meeting someone at an appointment whether male or female.

I sat down. He said, "Let me send this email." I watched as he finished typing.

He asked if I wanted something to drink, then got up to order and fetch it. OK, this guy has some manners.

We had an enjoyable conversation. After 90 minutes, the shop began closing. He said, "We need to go." I stood up, took my coat from the chair and donned it. He rose and stepped back from the table, which I thought was odd. Did he find me so odious he was stepping away? Was he scared of me? I said, "Give me a hug," which he did. He followed me to the door. I opened the door into the night.

Upon exiting, he said, "I'm parked over there," pointing in the opposite direction than my car. "I'm over there," I said. "It was nice to meet you," he said and turned to walk to his car.

It's been a long time since a man didn't offer to walk me to my car after dark.

So was this man without basic manners? Or was I expecting too much? I chocked it up to he wasn't into me and was doing only the minimal of niceties. My male friends tell me that when a man is into a woman, he'll put his hand out to take her coat when she reaches for it. He makes sure to open doors, and would always want just a few more minutes with her by walking her to her car to ensure she reached it safely. Heck, if he was into her, he'd say, "The coffee shop is closing. I'm enjoying our conversation. Would you like to continue over a bite to eat?"

However, when I arrived home he texted me that he enjoyed meeting me and liked our conversation. If he wasn't interested, why would he text? It was a non-committal text that didn't suggest another encounter. I responded to him that I liked our conversation, too, and he said he'd call me soon. I figured I'd never hear from him again.

> *If he wasn't interested, why would he text?*

Two days later, he texted then called. I said I was surprised to hear from him. He asked why, and I said I didn't think he was interested in me. He sounded incredulous and asked why. I pointed out the not walking to my car and the tepid follow-up text. He said he could see me walking to my car and saw I was safe.

I learned from a wise person to make sure the other person knows of your efforts, as they won't think you care if they don't know. That's not to say you should announce every nice thing you do for another, but make sure you say, "I filled up your gas tank" or "I made sure to get the brand of OJ you like" or "I hunted for two-toned flowers and finally found the ones you like."

(These are sort of lame examples, but I hope you get what I mean.)

So in dating, if you are attracted to someone you need to show it clearly, otherwise the person may not know.

What are your expectations of manners in dating? Do you give the other person a little slack on first meeting? Or do you think if s/he isn't conscious of manners at the very beginning it won't improve?

# *Do you suffer from verbal diarrhea?*

I had two dates recently with successful, nice, intelligent, educated men. However, I noticed something that I find extremely common in dating — they both had no idea they were droning on in great detail about people or stories that held nearly no interest for their listener (me!).

I work to be a generous listener, asking questions about people's lives and stories that show I'm interested. My questions are designed to uncover their values and interests. I am not perfect at it, of course. I realize some people are put off by too many questions, so it's important to interject tidbits from one's life as well.

However, the monologue disguised as conversation is such a rampant issue, it's been suggested that I lead a seminar on how to be a conscious conversationalist.

So allow me to share some ideas in hopes that these suggestions might be useful to those who want to increase their conversational prowess — thus increasing the likelihood of more dates with similar people.

Practice with a friend.

If you're serious about improving your conversational skill, do what you'd do with any skill you want to improve — practice and get feedback. Find a pal who also wants to improve and practice together.

> *Find a pal who also wants to improve and practice together.*

If you were in my workshop, I'd put you in pairs to find out about each other. I'd give each pair a stopwatch and ask you to track each other's speaking time. So if you and I are partners, when you started to talk I'd hit the stopwatch and stop it when you asked me a question. Then you'd start the stopwatch when I started talking.

If either of you went over 5 minutes without the other talking, the listener would say "stop." Then the talker could be aware that they are droning.

In this exercise you'd pause between turns to log the time each spent talking. At the end of the exercise you'd show each other the numbers. If one of you continually talked up to 5 minutes, then s/he needs to be more conscious of their monopolizing the time.

The goal of this exercise is not to "win" by having the lowest cumulative time. In fact, you could be a jerk and answer the other's questions with one- or two-word responses. That gets tiresome quickly. I recently stopped communicating with someone who asked me to text him and then he only responded with one-word answers. It was too much work to try to have a conversation. So I dropped it — and him.

Ask a question at the end of your sharing.

In emails, on the phone, or in person, work to end your comments with a question, even it's just mirroring back their question.

Person A: "Where were you born?"

Person B: "I was born in XXXX. Where did you grow up?"

A: What do you love about your job?"

B: "That's a good question. I love the flexibility, variety, good compensation and ability to see the world. What's your favorite part of your job?"

A: "Why are you divorced?"

B: "We realized we wanted different things in the future. What precipitated your break up?"

A: "Do you have kids?"

B: "Yes, I have 3 kids, all grown and out of the house. What about you?"

A: "What do you like to do for fun?"

B: "I like a variety of activities, including biking, hiking, dancing, theater, concerts, movies, trying new restaurants, cooking, gardening, reading and listening to NPR. What are some of your favorite recreational activities?"

If you already know his answer to the question he asked you, you can use this to either dig deeper into the question or switch topics.

As much as possible, try to avoid a preponderance of "reporting questions," e.g., "How was work?" "What did you have for lunch?" "Did you talk to your mom today?" unless there are extenuating circumstances that would make that question important (e.g., his mom recently moved to a nursing home and he'd shared his concern about her adjusting).

Get the other person to share equally.

In our workshop, you'd do an exercise I use in my seminars. I give each pair a potato — yes, really! This is a version of hot potato in that the goal is to get rid of the (pretend) very hot potato quickly. But you can only give it to the other person if you ask them a question.

So you want to make your answers pithy, without being curt, and ask them a question to pass on the potato to them with your question.

In the advanced version, we'd cover open-ended vs. closed-ended or limited-answer questions and how to avoid the latter. Why? Because closed-ended (generally beginning with who, what, where, when or how) get people to answer too briefly to get to know much about them. By asking open-ended questions/statements (tell me about, share with me, elaborate on, help me understand, as well as some how, what and even why questions), you get more information about the person.

Admit if you feel you've hogged the air time.

Simply say, "I've been talking nearly non-stop. I'd like to know more about you. Tell me, what do you love about your life?"

By practicing these ideas with a pal you can give each other feedback and kudos. Don't be afraid you'll feel stupid — when you're learning or improving any skill, you will, no doubt, do it poorly at first. Allow yourself to not be perfect, and just listen to the feedback and practice some more.

So, how have you learned to better your conversational skills? What do you know you could still improve on? (You knew I'd have to ask!)

# "It doesn't hurt to try"

You've heard this bromide from people who want to encourage others to be more bold, or to justify their own failed behavior.

So does it hold true in dating?

Yes, it doesn't hurt to try...

   ...to ask someone out for coffee who you've admired from afar, or even just met.

   ...to contact someone online who seems interesting.

   ...to show your interest in someone by asking about their life.

However, it does hurt to try...

   ...to kiss someone on the first date who hasn't given you very clear signals they are interested, and/ or who you haven't asked if you could. You could ruin any

*It does hurt to try.*

chance of a second date as you could be seen as overly aggressive and inappropriate.

...to get too physical too soon — a hand on a thigh or too touchy. You could be perceived as disrespectful and crossing the other's boundaries.

...to continue to pursue someone after they've said they aren't interested. You'll seem like you're ignoring their wishes and even stalking.

So while some trying something bold can be positive, other times it can be harmful.

When you hear yourself think, "It doesn't hurt to try," think through the options to see if it actually might hurt to try. If someone could respond negatively, seek alternatives.

# Resources

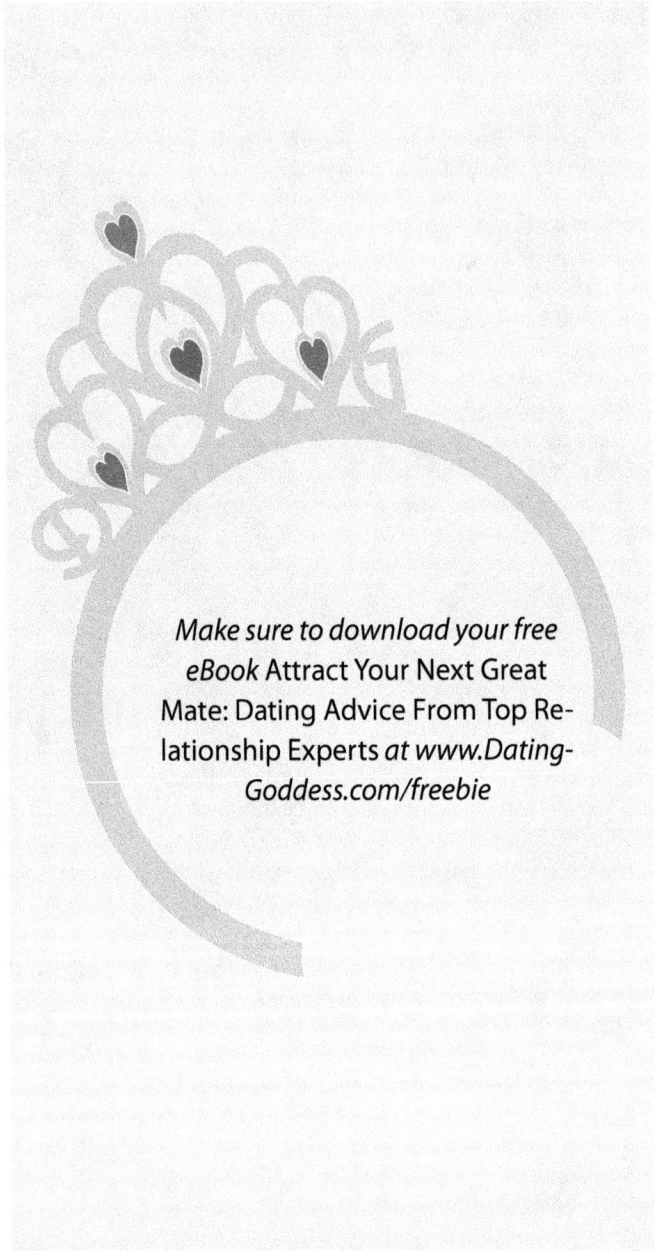

*Make sure to download your free eBook* Attract Your Next Great Mate: Dating Advice From Top Relationship Experts *at www.DatingGoddess.com/freebie*

# *Afterword*

At the time of this writing, I have not yet found my true King Charming. I continue my search with verve. I've become more discerning about what I want and don't want. I've met some wonderful men pals — my treasures — who continue to be in touch.

I wish you much luck in your adventure. It will be fun and frustrating, exhilarating and exasperating, and sexy or sexless. So much depends on you, your approach and your attitude. My books are designed to help you enjoy as much as possible and ward off unpleasantness. But nearly all adventures have wonderful highs as well as a few lows. If you know that going in and arm yourself with information on what to expect, you'll have more of the positives and fewer of the negatives.

Please drop by www.DatingGoddess.com and join in the discussion and report on your experiences.

Dating Goddess

# *Resources*

o to www.datinggoddess.com to access a variety of useful resources. We work to suggest resources we think have value.

## Dating and relationship book reviews

These reviews will save you time and money as I've given you my take on specific books, CDs and more. Some are worth your effort to buy and read or listen to them — some are not. We're always adding new book reviews, so check frequently. We'll also notify our mailing list when new resources are added.

## Dating site links

There are a lot of dating sites on the Internet. I've listed the ones I think are worth investigating.

## Dating products and tools

Dating can be daunting. We're continually looking at

ways to make it easier and more fun. We'll provide info on games, tools, even date-wear that will help others know you're available, or help you get to know potential suitors better.

## Dating and relationship advice sites

Advice "experts" abound on the Internet as anyone can self-proclaim themseves as expert — even if they haven't dated in 30 years and never in midlife. I've worked to find experts who's advice I generally think is solid.

## Midlife recources

We'll feature Web sites, books, events and other resources we think might interest you.

## Newly discovered resources

I'll add other resources as we discover them, subscribe to our mailing list to get the scoop as soon as we find them. Go to www.DatingGoddess.com to register for our mailing list. Don't worry, we won't sell or give your email to anyone.

# Acknowledgments

et me start by acknowledging the 112 men who helped trigger the lessons contained in this book. Some prompted several! They remain nameless here to protect their identity, although most would recognize references to them. Plus the thousands more whose winks, emails and calls didn't result in a date, but helped me learn the dating game. And all those men who I emailed who never responded — such a blessing to have them weed themselves out.

> I acknowledge
> the 112 men
> who triggered
> my lessons

I'd like to thank my Seven Sisters mastermind group for the tremendous brainstorming, noodling, strategizing and encouragement. I wouldn't have begun this project without the prodding of Val Cade, Chris Clarke-Epstein, Mariah Burton Nelson, Sue Dyer, Sam Horn and Marilynn Mobley.

Thank you to my good friends who've listened to my dating stories ad nauseam, and whose support and wisdom are embedded in this text. Ed Betts, Ken Braly, Bruce Daley, Tom Drews, Elaine Floyd, Paulette Ensign, Scott Friedman, Craig Harrison, Mary Jansen, Tom Johnson, Sandy Jones, Mary Kilkenny, Ellie Klevins, Patrick Lynch, Mary Marcdante, Barbara McNichol, Ann Peterson, Anthony Ramsey, Caterina Rando, Kristy Rogers, Jana Stanfield, Holly Steil, Terry Tepliz, and George Walther, thank you.

# The Adventures in Delicious Dating After 40 series

The Adventures in Delicious Dating After 40 series is designed to help you understand your own midlife dating journey. It is not a road map, as we all take different routes. It is a guide to help you understand yourself, midlife men, and the dating process. Hopefully, you'll not only learn from the lessons and insights shared in this series, but you'll examine how they apply — or don't — to your own dating adventure.

You'll get the scoop on what you need to know, what's changed since you last dated, and how to navigate inevitable bumps in the road.

Following is an overview of each book in the series and a sampling of some of the chapter titles. All are detailed at www.DatingGoddess.com.

## *Date or Wait: Are You Ready for Mr. Great?*

Are you ready for a special man in your life? You have a great life. But you know you'd like a special man to share it. You think you're ready to date, but you haven't done it in a while.

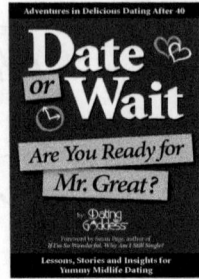

What should you consider before you actually start dating full bore? Even if you've reentered the dating world, this will give you a foundation of attitude and philosophy to make your adventure more fulfilling.

Sample chapters

♥ From hurt to flirt

♥ Dating is like Baskin-Robbins

♥ You've got to kiss a lot of…princes!

♥ What's your definition of dating success?

♥ Are you open to receiving?

♥ Dating: A self-designed personal-growth workshop

♥ Hands-on dating research

♥ Being present to the presents

♥ Being aggressively single

♥ Approaching dating like a buffet

♥ Is Brad Pitt ruining your love life?

♥ Treasures can come in dented packages

## *Assessing Your Assets: Why You're A Great Catch*

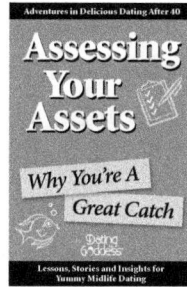

You have many wonderful qualities. But it's easy to focus on one's flaws — at least what seem like flaws to you. However, to the right man your imperfections are endearing, attractive and lovable. You have to be clear what you offer a man who will find you enchanting.

*Assessing Your Assets* helps you look at what you bring to a new relationship. It will help you see your good points so you'll approach dating with more confidence.

Sample chapters

💜 Don't think you are damaged goods

💜 You are (probably) more attractive than you think!

💜 They aren't called "hate handles"

💜 Are you a good man picker?

💜 What are your deal breakers?

💜 Are you arguing your limitations?

💜 Turn your liabilities into assets

💜 The strong vs. nice woman debate

💜 Is your sense of humor stunting your dating?

💜 Why are we drawn to bad boys?

💜 The zest test

## In Search of King Charming: Who Do I Want to Share My Throne?

You are no longer looking for "Prince" Charming because you are a queen. You want someone who is at your level, not groveling at your feet. You want a king — someone who's your equal and with whom you can rule the throne together!

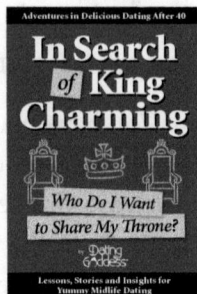

This book focuses on helping you better define what you want beyond tall, dark and handsome! You'll consider characteristics you might not have thought of before. You'll look at what you want now.

Sample chapters

💚 Building your Franken-boyfriend

💚 What's your "perfect boyfriend's" job description?

💚 A man to go with your wardrobe

💚 In search of the elusive good kisser

💚 When you're clear on what you want, it appears

💚 Are you dating the same guy in different bodies?

💚 Does he fit in your world?

💚 What's your kissing quotient?

💚 Is your guy's loving muscle strong?

💚 Do you both have the same dating rhythm?

## *Embracing Midlife Men: Insights Into Curious Behaviors*

Do you sometimes scratch your head after interacting with a midlife man, wondering, "What could he possibly be thinking?" Especially if it's before, during or after a date with a man who presumably wants to impress you!

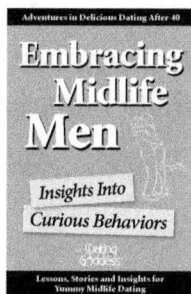

This book focuses on better understanding midlife men's behaviors. When you grasp what's going on in his head it's much easier to embrace him. Men are wondrous creatures, so we need to understand them better and love them for who they are.

Sample chapters

💜 Men are like shoes

💜 Why men disappear when it gets serious

💜 Chivalry isn't dead —but it seems to be hibernating

💜 Do men want feisty women?

💜 Midlife men have forgotten how to date

💜 Are you getting prime time from your man?

💜 When a man tells you what he paid for things

💜 Does he treat you like his ex?

💜 Has Greg Behrendt done women a disservice?

💜 Tales of woo

## Dipping Your Toe in the Dating Pool: Dive In Without Belly Flopping

You've decided you are ready — you want to start dating. Maybe you've already had a few coffee dates with several men. You want to be as successful as possible on your dating adventure.

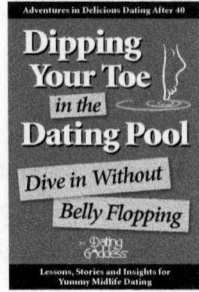

This book focuses on getting started on your dating adventures. We cover what you need to know as you begin your journey.

Sample chapters

- Do you have the right datewear?
- Dating with integrity
- Building your rejection muscle
- When "be yourself" is questionable advice
- Faux beaus and practice dating
- Are you making bad decisions out of loneliness?
- Being "in wonder" about your date's behavior
- When do you feel most vulnerable in dating?
- Are you out of his league — or he yours?
- Why listening is so seductive

## *Winning at the Online Dating Game: Stack the Deck in Your Favor*

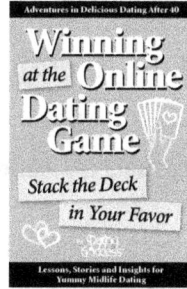

Internet dating can be frustrating or fruitful. It will be much less exasperating if you know how to read and weed out men's profiles that aren't appropriate for you. And you'll have a steady stream of potential suitors if you know how to write a compelling profile for yourself.

This book focuses on the ins and outs of online dating. How to play the game, which has it's own rules and language. If you don't understand how online dating works, you'll waste a lot of time connecting with men who are not a possible fit for you.

Sample chapters

💜 Shopping for men

💜 Safe online dating

💜 Is 21st Century dating unnatural?

💜 What do men look at in your profile?

💜 Euphemisms uncovered

💜 Are you describing yourself compellingly?

💜 No, I will not be dating your Harley

💜 Playing the online dating game

💜 Scantily clothed pictures

## Check Him Out Before Going Out: Avoiding Dud Dates

Under the cloak of the anonymity that email and the phone provides, men often reveal more than they intend. If you ask the right questions you can find out a lot about his values and view of the world after just an interaction or two.

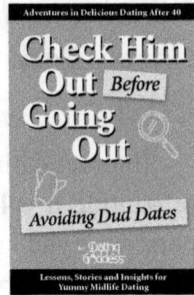

This book focuses on what you need to ask before agreeing to even a coffee date. You need to vet the men who email and call you to ensure you're not likely to waste your time with men who clearly aren't a match.

Sample chapters

💜 Becoming smitten with the fantasy

💜 Can Google help — or hinder — your dating life?

💜 Qualify your potential dates before meeting

💜 The art of consideration

💜 Anticipating a big date is like awaiting Santa

💜 Being seduced by what he is over who he is

💜 Are you his spare?

💜 My boyfriend, whom I haven't met

💜 When canceling is the right thing to do

💜 Politics, religion and sex — oh my!

## First-Rate First Dates: Increasing the Chances of a Second Date

You can tell a lot about someone within the first 30 minutes. What does he talk about? Does he ask you questions? If so, what does he want to know about you? What do you need to know about him? How does he treat you? How does he treat those around you?

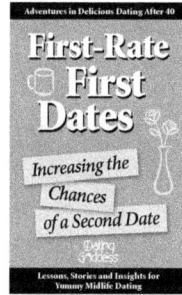

This book focuses on what goes on during the first date. How do you determine if you want a second date? What you can do to increase the likelihood your date will ask you for a second? That is if you want a repeat!

Sample chapters

💚 Start with coffee

💚 How do you greet him?

💚 When it clicks, throw out some of your criteria

💚 Tracking your date's score

💚 Clues a guy is just looking for a booty call

💚 12 signs he won't be asking for a second date

💚 First-date red flags that this guy isn't for you

💚 Honesty is not always the best policy

💚 Chemistry, or does he make my toes curl?

💚 Women's first-date blunders

## *Real Deal or Faux Beau: Should You Keep Seeing Him?*

You've begun to go out with a man you like. How do you decide if you should continue seeing him, or if you should release him because he's not The One?

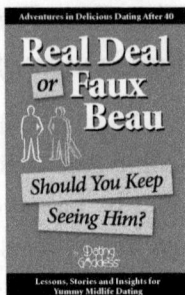

This book focuses on second dates and beyond. During the dating process you are both assessing if you want to keep seeing each other. This book helps you determine what questions you need to ask yourself.

Sample chapters

💚 Deciding to see him again or not

💚 What's your date's Delight/Disappointment Scale score?

💚 Broaching tough conversations

💚 "I want to respect me in the morning"

💚 Does he invite you to his place?

💚 Are you stingy in dating?

💚 When his hand is on your knee too soon

💚 Easy way to ask hard questions

💚 Rose-colored glasses obscure red flags

💚 If his stories don't add up, subtract yourself

## *Multidating Responsibly: Play the Field Without Being A Player*

Playing the field is frowned on in some circles. There are definitely appropriate and inappropriate ways to date several men simultaneously.

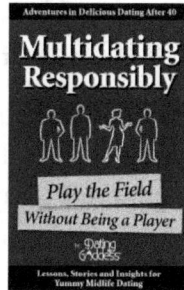

This book focuses on how to date around responsibly and with integrity without leading men on. If you do it with honesty, you can date several people at once until you're both ready to focus only on each other.

Sample chapters

💜 "Pimpin'" — Dating multiple guys

💜 Multi-dating pros and cons

💜 Your Date-A-Base — tracking multiple suitors

💜 "Hot bunking" your beaus

💜 Are you a "Let's Make a Deal" type of dater?

💜 Assume there are other women

💜 Dating's revolving door

💜 How long do you hedge your bet?

💜 Beware of multi-tasking when multi-dating

💜 Back burner beaus

💜 The boyfriend phone

## Moving On Gracefully: Break Up Without Heartache

"Breaking up" sounds so high school, doesn't it? But part of the dating process is saying something when one of you decides not to date the other anymore. Going "poof" is not a mature or respectful option in midlife.

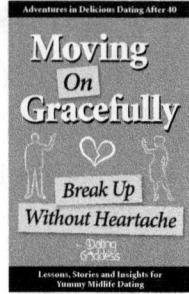

This book focuses on surviving a breakup, whether you initiate it or not. Either way, it's never easy to break up if you have developed any fondness toward the other.

Sample chapters

💚 Hello — goodbye: How to say no thanks after meeting

💚 Releasing back into the dating pool

💚 50 ways to leave your lover? 4 ways not to leave your suitor

💚 Breaking up is hard to do — right

💚 Why men go "poof"

💚 How to trump being dumped

💚 When breaking up is a "Get Out of Jail Free" card

💚 How to detect the end is near

💚 Failed relationships' blessings

💚 He's broken up with you — he just didn't tell you

💚 Rejection is protection

### *From Fear to Frolic: Get Naked Without Getting Embarrassed*

This book focuses on what you need to consider and know before getting physically intimate with a man you're dating. This is nerve-wracking to many midlife women. This book will prepare you.

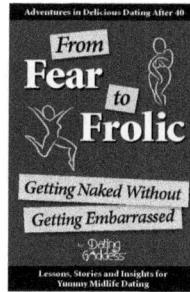

Sample chapters

💜 Sleepover do's and don'ts

💜 Does he want in your life — or just in your bedroom?

💜 Getting naked with him the first time

💜 An excuse to seduce or how important is bedroom bliss?

💜 What to ask yourself before getting naked with him

💜 Are you and your guy on the same sexual time line?

💜 Sharing your sexual owner's manual with him

💜 What women need from a man before having sex

💜 Why too-soon midlife sex is like non-fat food

💜 How dating sex is like waffles

💜 Too-soon seduction: "I'm special, but not THAT special"

## Ironing Out Dating Wrinkles: Work Through Challenges Without Getting Steamed

Nearly all relationships have some ups and downs. Part of getting to know someone is knowing how they work through relationship misunderstandings.

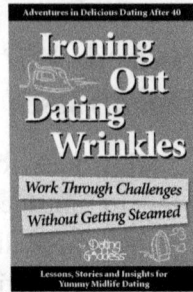

This book focuses on how to work through the inevitable hiccups that happen when you are getting to know each other. If you can both deal with challenges, the bond deepens and you find yourself smitten.

Sample chapters

💜 When your guy vexes you, ask what your highest self would do

💜 The first fight

💜 You want boo; he wants boo-ty

💜 Where's the line between getting your needs met and being selfish?

💜 Expressing your upset with your guy

💜 Is his toothbrush in your cabinet too soon?

💜 Do you love how he loves you?

💜 Is he collecting data on how to make you happy?

💜 Be careful of being smitten

💜 Exclusivity: How and when to broach it